once we were
strangers

"*Once We Were Strangers* offers a glimpse into the bridge-building, fear-silencing, life-affirming gift of cross-cultural friendship. This is an important and timely message. I highly recommend that you read this book and step into the transformative process of loving your neighbors."

Peter Greer, president and CEO, HOPE
International; coauthor of *Rooting for Rivals*

"In this gentle, compelling story, Shawn Smucker brings an ongoing tragedy many of us only experience in the headlines vividly to life. This intimate portrayal of a friendship is at a time when too many fear 'the other' in their midst. Smucker's emotionally rich portrayal of a friendship with a Syrian refugee and his family is illuminating—and necessary."

Anne Bogel, author of *I'd Rather Be Reading:
The Delights and Dilemmas of the Reading Life*

"We humans are hardwired to best learn through story. I can't imagine anyone *not* learning through Shawn's storytelling the truths about what it means to live in community with our neighbors, to understand how differences sometimes overshadow our vastly larger similarities, to be at home, and ultimately, to be human. This story needs to be told—and then? It needs to be replicated in some way throughout all our communities. I'm grateful Shawn has shared his story with us."

Tsh Oxenreider, author of *At Home in the World:
Reflections on Belonging While Wandering the Globe*

"As politicians turn their backs on the suffering people of Syria, this compassionate journey into a refugee's experiences is what the church needs to stir us into action so that we can rediscover what it means to act justly and to love mercy among those who are suffering. I hope that every church in America will own a copy of this book."

Ed Cyzewski, author of *Flee, Be Silent, Pray:
An Anxious Evangelical Finds Peace with
God through Contemplative Prayer*

once we were strangers

strangers

What Friendship with a Syrian Refugee
Taught Me about Loving My Neighbor

SHAWN SMUCKER

Revell

a division of Baker Publishing Group
Grand Rapids, Michigan

Published by Revell
a division of Baker Publishing Group
PO Box 6287, Grand Rapids, MI 49516-6287
www.revellbooks.com

Printed in the United States of America

Library of Congress Cataloging-in-Publication Data
Names: Smucker, Shawn, author.
Title: Once we were strangers : what friendship with a Syrian refugee taught me
    about loving my neighbor / Shawn Smucker.
Description: Grand Rapids, MI : Revell, a division of Baker Publishing Group,
    [2018]
Identifiers: LCCN 2018017117 | ISBN 9780800734763 (pbk. : alk. paper)
Subjects: LCSH: Friendship—Religious aspects—Christianity. | Smucker,
    Shawn. | Refugees—Syria. | Christianity and other religions—Islam. |
    Islam—Relations—Christianity.
Classification: LCC BV4647.F7 S68 2018 | DDC 277.48/15083092 [B] —dc23
LC record available at https://lccn.loc.gov/2018017117

18 19 20 21 22 23 24   7 6 5 4 3 2 1

In keeping with biblical principles of creation stewardship, Baker Publishing Group advocates the responsible use of our natural resources. As a member of the Green Press Initiative, our company uses recycled paper when possible. The text paper of this book is composed in part of post-consumer waste.

To everyone far from home

Contents

No one leaves home
unless home is the mouth of a shark.

Warsan Shire, "Home"

Part One

The Friend

One day an expert in religious law stood up to test Jesus by asking him this question: "Teacher, what should I do to inherit eternal life?"

Jesus replied, "What does the law of Moses say? How do you read it?"

The man answered, "'You must love the LORD your God with all your heart, all your soul, all your strength, and all your mind.' And, 'Love your neighbor as yourself.'"

"Right!" Jesus told him. "Do this and you will live!"

The man wanted to justify his actions, so he asked Jesus, "And who is my neighbor?"

Luke 10:25–29

1

Two Grains of Sand

November 2016

The stories of other people are always hidden from us at first, waiting in the shadows. They are tentative, skittish things, these hidden tales, frightened of what might become of them if they step out into the light. When I first met Mohammad, there were things I never could have guessed about him, things I never could have imagined.

The man rides his motorcycle through the Syrian countryside, his wife and four sons somehow balanced on the bike with him. He has received a tip that his village will soon be bombed. Their combined weight wobbles the motorcycle from side to side, and he shouts at them to hold still, hold still.

The man sits quietly on a friend's porch, drinking very dark coffee, watching bombs rain down on his village miles away. "That was your house," he says, then, ten minutes later, "I think that one hit my house." He takes another sip of coffee. His children play in the yard.

The man walks through the pitch-black Syrian wilderness, his family in a line behind him. He can feel the tension in his wife, the fear in his older boys. Someone ahead shouts, "Get down!" and they all collapse into the dust, holding their breath, trying to keep the baby quiet. There is the taste of dirt. There are rocks digging into his body. There is the sound of his boys, afraid, so far from home.

"Abba," they whimper. "Abba."

There are nearly 6,000 miles between Mohammad's hometown and Lancaster, Pennsylvania. There are dozens of other countries he could have been relocated to. Hundreds of other cities. Yet somehow he came here, less than a mile from my house, to the area where my ancestors have lived for the last 250 years.

Imagine two grains of sand drawing closer together. The waves crash, stirring them up; the current pushes, the undertow pulls. There is the swirl of fish swimming past, shells dragging along the bottom, scraping out trenches. Then, at some particular point in time, these two grains of sand lift, rise toward the light, come into contact.

What are the odds of these crossings?

Where in this world will we find each other?

2

Help

November 14, 2016

I park my car along the sidewalk in front of our Lancaster row home, the streetlights glowing yellow, the intersection empty. The crossing signal changes. But no cars drive south through the green light on Prince Street—it's after midnight, and our small city sleeps.

The air is cold outside the car, and I pull my shoulders up and fumble with the keys, trying to unlock the front door and get inside as quickly as possible. I glance to the left and the right before going in, seeing a long row of porches in each direction, vacant and displaying a wide variety of city life. To the left, nice porches with nice furniture and nice rugs laid out under nice iron porch lights. To the right, a foreclosed home with a broken porch swing, and beyond that a row home turned into apartments covered in dust and leaves. A dark alley.

One of the doors opens a few houses down to the right, and a man walks out, shivering. He cups his hands and lights a cigarette, the orange glow pushing against the shadows. He glances over, appearing surprised to see me, and I give him a wave, a nod. He waves back with the hand that holds the cigarette, and it makes an arc of ember through the night. I nod again and smile, push open the door, and go inside.

Walking in, I consider, as I often do late at night, how hard it is to believe there are six children and a wife asleep in this house. The living room is still, a blanket draped over the sofa, pillows on the floor. The hallway is quiet until I walk through it, the hundred-year-old floorboards creaking and moaning under my feet. I briefly consider continuing into the kitchen, but I am so tired; instead, I head straight up the stairs.

I peek into our oldest son's room—his teenage body stretches diagonally across the small bed, his head under the covers. It's cold in that back bedroom with its old windows and the door that leads outside onto the small porch. I walk through the dark and feel the radiators, make sure they're on. Steaming hot to the touch.

The hall light is on and it shines into our bedroom. I undress and pull back the covers and find our second youngest, Leo, curled up in a ball on my side of the bed. Sam, our middle son, is asleep on the floor. Children are everywhere, and I smile. This is a normal night in our house.

I pick up Leo and carry him to his bed in the neighboring room. He is limp the entire time, deep in sleep. Deciding to check on everyone else while I'm awake, I make the rounds, including the third floor, looking in on our daughters. Everyone is asleep.

I, on the other hand, am now wide awake. Hoping that sleep will sneak up on me, I go back to the bedroom, step carefully over Sam, and crawl into bed beside my wife, Maile. I try not to wake her, pulling up the covers in slow motion, holding my breath, trying to move slowly so as not to shake the bed, but she is always aware of my arriving.

"Hey," she says in a quiet voice without opening her eyes, reaching over to hold my hand. We lie there quietly, the stillness of the house all around us.

"How was your night?" she asks in a weak voice.

"Not bad for a Monday," I say. "Pretty busy. I guess when it's this cold, no one wants to walk anywhere."

"I worry about you," she says, her eyes now open. "I worry when you're out driving this late."

"Don't worry," I say, turning toward her, pushing the hair out of her eyes. "There's nothing to worry about."

A car goes by outside, the headlights pushing a window-shaped block of light across the wall. Somewhere in the distance, a siren wails. The hospital is only two blocks away. We hear a lot of sirens on that street.

Just when I think Maile has fallen back asleep, her voice eases into the stillness. "Are you still going to Church World Service tomorrow?"

"Yeah, in the afternoon. Does that work okay with your schedule?"

"I think so. Are you still meeting with the Syrian man, the one you might want to write a book with?"

"Yeah. Mohammad."

"That should be interesting."

"I hope so," I say, smiling.

She smiles at me and rolls over, facing away. I turn away too, facing the window. Our backs are against each other. Our cold feet touch.

"It's important work, you know," she says, and I can tell by the sound of her voice that sleep is coming for her. It's just outside the bedroom door, peeking inside. It's coming across the room, the floorboards creaking.

"I just want to help," I say. "I don't know what else to do."

I just want to help. I think briefly about those words, that sentiment. Would writing a book, would getting this man's story bound and published and sold, help? How? Who?

"I guess we'll see," I say, as if in answer to my own concerns, but Maile does not reply. She's asleep. I can hear Sam's heavy breathing coming up to me from the floor beside the bed. Another car drives by, and someone's car alarm goes off for five or ten seconds, and a cold wind shakes the house.

3

The Question

October 11, 2012

Mohammad couldn't rid himself of the question. He tried to ignore it. He had busied himself during the day with work and helped his customers, but his irritation had spilled into his interactions with his wife and children. His attempts at looking away from the question made him short-tempered. That evening, as he closed up the small market he operated out of his home, as he counted his money and looked over his inventory, the question had become even more consuming. He wanted to think of anything else, but there it was, stuck in his mind like a speck of dust in his eye, irritating, unable to be ignored.

On the evening of October 11, 2012, Mohammad kick-started his motorcycle and buzzed out onto the local streets, his face expressionless, flat. Uncertain. He lived in Um Walad, a small village in the district of Dara'a, Syria, about 450 miles south of

Aleppo. The largest city in their region also went by the name of Dara'a.

Normally Mohammad felt a strong sense of relief when he headed out on his motorcycle. Flying down those unpaved roads usually gave him the feeling that he could breathe again.

But on that night, relief didn't come. The question was now at the forefront of his mind, and he marinated on it, turned it over and over in his mind. Irritated, he punched the throttle and drove faster than he should have. But no matter how fast he went, no matter how far he rode, the question was there in front of him, just beyond the single beam of his headlight.

How many people have already fled Um Walad?

He clenched and unclenched his jaw as he drove, his eyes scanning the village, the houses far apart. He was going nowhere in particular.

So far, he didn't like what he saw. He didn't like the answer that was presenting itself.

The houses were separated by expansive fields. This was what he referred to as his village. In the summer, those fields were a lush green, covered in wheat and chickpeas, but by the time fall arrived, they were a deep, earthy brown. This was the same village where he had been born, the same village where his father had grown up. A few tufts of vegetation fought their way up, and the rows upon rows of olive trees still had their leaves, but besides that, the endless stretch of flat land was barren.

The southern border of the Dara'a region ran up against Jordan, where millions of his countrymen had already fled in order to escape the Syrian civil war that was flaring into something unexpected, something terrifying. The wilderness that separated the Syrian villages from one another and eventually from Jordan was largely uninhabited. It was a rocky wilderness, the color of light suede, and mountains rose up, always on the distant horizon, harsh and forbidding.

The cool night air danced around him as he rode, flapping the sleeves on his short-sleeved shirt and blasting against his hair. The farther he drove, the more anxious he felt. Dust kicked up behind him as he went from one cluster of houses to the next. The houses were a mishmash of cement block, sometimes covered in stucco or corrugated metal, sometimes bare block. Darkness gathered, and his headlight seemed to grow brighter. The light bounced and jerked as he crested another small hill, then another. The more streets he turned down, the faster his heart raced.

Nearly everyone was gone. This was the answer he had dreaded.

The previous year had ushered in a new time in Syria, a time full of things Mohammad could hardly believe were happening. Everyone in his village had heard the gossip spreading, news from the capital that the conflict there was getting worse between the people and the police. The army had become involved. Rumors swirled about the government imprisoning people and even executing them if they didn't walk the line.

Who would have dreamed this only a year or two ago, when they were happily living in a peaceful Syria, running a small grocery out of their home, the boys running through the countryside, a new baby in the house? Who could have seen this coming when he was young and a driver in Kuwait, or when he first visited teenage Moradi as a suitor, or when he was dancing with the other men of the village at their wedding? Who could have guessed this when his oldest three boys were born, one after the other, their happy cries filling the house? He had never seen war, not in his lifetime. To him, Syria was a beautiful country full of olive groves and long stretches of quiet wilderness, a country of neighbors and family. To him, it was home.

By the time he went on his motorcycle ride that night, he had heard too many alarming stories, and the rumors were impossible to separate from the truth. The capital was under a government siege, and people were running out of food. Was it true? Some of his friends had even gone all the way to Aleppo or to neighboring cities to try to help their family members get food, to break through the various blockades and ensure their family did not starve. But the government wouldn't let anyone in, and they forced people to stay in their homes. The economy was crashing. There were few jobs. There was less food.

Things had not reached this point in Mohammad's village, but because some of the villagers had been involved in activities against the government, his village had been bombed. And people had started to leave.

How did I not see it before now? he thought, bouncing along the road.

He supposed it had all happened gradually. First this family, then that family. First one house abandoned, then another. He was a busy man at market, putting in long hours, and somehow he hadn't noticed the vacant streets, the empty sidewalks, the lack of children. He had fled their village for days at a time with his family while the government sent down shells indiscriminately. They would go to the neighboring village for an afternoon or a day or several days. He guessed that people simply were not returning. When people leave slowly, when a village's death is spread out over months or years, and when many of these people leave in the middle of the night—when they simply walk into the wilderness—it is easy to miss the signs.

"What am I doing?" he mumbled as he turned his motorcycle toward home. During his entire trip that night, he had seen only two people walking from here to there.

Two people.

"Why have I waited so long?" he asked himself, thinking of his wife and sons. He revved the accelerator, speeding home. He arrived long after dark, but even then, he could see the splintered telephone pole beside his house. It looked like a giant's frayed toothpick, evidence that the government's mortars were falling too close—this one had hit less than a month ago.

"Why have I waited so long?" he muttered again.

———

Late on the following morning, October 12, Mohammad came inside after working for only a few hours. He knew it was time. They would tell only their parents.

Bursting through the front door, he found his wife. "It's time," he said. "We need to go."

"Are you sure?" she asked.

"I'm sure," he said. "Everyone is gone. There is nothing here for us."

She nodded. "I'll get the boys," she said.

Mohammad found some things they could carry their food and water in: backpacks, satchels, a plastic bag. He raided the cupboards and filled the bags with as much as he thought his young boys could carry on their backs. He glanced nervously out the windows. Only weeks before, his friend had been struck on the hand by shrapnel as everyone had fled to a nearby Christian village to avoid a government air raid.

Mohammad's property had been hit three times in recent weeks. Every time he walked inside, he saw the large patch of cement on the wall, his attempt at filling in the hole the bomb had left. He stared at it that morning. That had been the last thing he could take. Constantly seeing the evidence of their danger right there inside their home, looking over their shoulder every evening while they ate, had spurred him on to his nighttime motorcycle ride to see how many people remained.

Syria was no longer a place to raise children—it had no future that Mohammad could see. Bashar al-Assad, president of Syria, had proven he would rather destroy everything than relinquish even the smallest shred of power. Everything was gone or going. It seemed that there could not be peace anymore. There could not be a quiet life. It wasn't safe.

He looked up as his wife entered the room, the children flooding in around her, excited to be doing something different, something out of the ordinary.

Mohammad stared at his four sons. His future. His everything. "We're going for a long walk tonight," he said. "You need to be strong. Brave."

They were ten, eight, four, and two years old. During the previous months, whenever they went outside, he always wondered if he would see them again. He knew they were doing the right thing by leaving. It was a relief to have made the decision. It was a relief to finally be doing something, instead of waiting, waiting, waiting for circumstances to change or the war to end or another bomb to hit their house.

"Hurry, hurry," he said. "The driver will be here soon."

4

Babel

November 15, 2016

I park my car along King Street, the main east-west boulevard that runs through Lancaster in central Pennsylvania, and I step out into a day too warm to be autumn. But there are red and gold leaves blowing around on the sidewalks, some of them crackling under my feet, and white clouds scoot across the sky. I wipe the sweat from my forehead with my forearm and wait for a gap in the traffic, then jog across King Street to the glass doors that lead into Church World Service's Lancaster office.

One week has passed since the United States elected Donald Trump as the forty-fifth president. There are still political signs everywhere: along the sidewalks, staked in grass, tied to iron railings, even mounted on the back of cars and pickup trucks. Some have come off their wire holders and are blowing in the street, swept along by the traffic. There is a lingering sense of disbelief at the result, a sort of relief that the endless campaigning is finally over, and, in the city and specifically among the refugee population, a palpable dread of what the future might hold for them and their families.

The reception area at CWS is warm and full of bodies, fuller than I've ever seen it, and I can't help but wonder if this is an early result of the election. I can certainly sense the urgency. It verges on panic. Languages, languages, languages fill the air, words leaping and darting and writhing here and there, words I've never heard before in tongues I cannot recognize, long strings of words that spin strange tales. Opening the glass door to the lobby at CWS is like walking into a miniature United Nations meeting. The crowd must shift as I enter the room in order to make more space. People look up at me, nod a quick hello, and when they realize I am not family or a CWS employee, their eyes dart back to the ground.

The seats are all full of Middle Eastern and African and Eastern European and Asian and Hispanic men and women, and there is a long line to talk to the receptionist. One man, small with pitch-black skin and gray hair, talks quickly and quietly into a telephone mounted on the wall. He is clearly frustrated. He sighs. He hangs up and, without taking his hand off the phone, picks up and redials. He begins again. He waits for a new connection.

A woman stands in the corner with two children, her voice sharp, her knuckles gripping them by the tender pieces of flesh just above the elbows. In her I recognize mothers I have seen in every culture, mothers trying to keep their children in line, like riders holding closely to the bit. The children, too, are familiar to me: as their mother scolds them, they try not to laugh. I grin and then look away. I don't want to encourage their dissent, bringing down an even greater wrath on their heads. But they are cute, and I see my own children there.

Despite the all-too-familiar humanity, I feel out of place in the midst of people whose needs are so pressing, so great. They need translators and jobs and a place to live. They need green cards and extensions for their visas and someone who can explain their children's homework. They need someone who can tell them that this new administration does not mean their extended families, still trapped in refugee tent cities overseas, will lose their ability to come to the US, that they will not have to start the two- or three- or four-year process over again.

I remember the Palestinian woman I met only a few months before, a Muslim woman who had fled Palestine, seeking asylum in the United States. I met her in the park with my wife and children, and the kids ran off to play on the swings while she told us how she was beaten by the police in her country for blogging about women's rights. At first she was reserved, hesitant to share. But as we sat in the warm sunshine, she opened up and the story came out to us. She revealed a world I found hard to comprehend, a world where people have to choose either staying with their spouses and children and facing execution or fleeing to a faraway country alone. She waits for her husband and children to get permission to join her. A year has already passed.

But it is the plight of the Syrians that compels me. There must be something else I can do. They have been in the news all summer, the bombing of the residents of Aleppo spread across our newsfeeds. Children covered in plaster and dust and blood. Children jumping cannonball-style into bomb craters filled with water in the middle of their city streets, the holes now being used as impromptu swimming pools. Children talking about the death of their entire families as if discussing the weather. It leaves a tangled ache in my chest, these videos of children. I have six children at home. I see them there among the tiny, hungry faces. I see them there, bleeding.

For weeks I dreamed of entire cities filled with buildings devoid of glass, all the windows blown out. I run from who knows what. I can never run fast enough.

———

I look around the CWS waiting room again. They need so much. Here in Lancaster, the county where my ancestors have lived for fourteen generations, I am surrounded by family, too many for me to even know them all. My wife makes fun of me because we go to a party and I end up meeting a second cousin for the first time. I am, in other words, surrounded by resources. By more than enough.

Standing there in the lobby, caught up in a whirlwind of need, I feel a twinge of guilt at my excess. I hope the others can't see it on me.

"Hello, Shawn?" a quiet, firm voice says, and I'm surprised to hear words in a language I understand. I'm even more surprised to hear my own name. I turn around, and Bilal rises up out of his seat like a bear out of a cave at the end of its hibernation. He is a large man, a gentle Iraqi I met only a few weeks ago, referred to me as a potential Arabic translator. He smiles, offering his huge hand. My fingers vanish in his friendly greeting.

"Bilal!" I say, smiling. "Thanks for meeting me here. Have you seen Stephanie?" Stephanie is our contact at CWS, someone I met when I was doing some volunteer work for them.

"No, no," he says. "I was waiting for you."

We talk about how busy it is in the reception area of CWS. We talk about how warm the weather is for November. We do not talk politics, at least not right away. I ask him about Iraq, what it's like this time of year. He has soft brown eyes and is very accommodating. We edge away from the front desk, toward the back of the room and the locked door that leads into the offices of CWS. We begin hesitantly talking about the recent election, each of us trying to feel out where the other stands, when a voice interrupts us.

"Shawn?"

I turn around. It's Stephanie, a young woman with brown hair and a wide smile. She moves the way someone moves when they have a lot to do: efficiently, without waste. I know she's taking time out of a busy day to help me.

"Hi, Stephanie," I say, shaking her hand. "It's good to see you again."

Bilal and I fall into line and follow her into the depths of CWS. The babble of voices, the cacophony of languages, goes quiet when the door slams behind us.

"Busy day?" I ask.

She nods and shrugs. "Busy day," she says, but I can tell by the way she says it that this is no busy day. This is no extraordinary day. This is the hectic busyness of all her days. This is every waking hour, when you are helping people flee from war or famine, when you are helping people come from all around the world, trying to help them find a safe place. You do what you can, and then you do a little bit more, and then you go home and try to sleep at night. I know this is how it goes. Don't ask me how I know. I just do.

I ask her about how the election results might impact them.

She gives me a sideways glance and sighs. "We have a lot of work to do." She shrugs again. "No one knows exactly how this will impact the refugees, not yet. There are a lot of families in the pipeline scheduled to arrive in the next few months—Syrians, Iraqis. We're concerned for them. We're concerned for the families who haven't started the process yet. We hope that those who have already been given permission to come will still be allowed to enter. Beyond that, who knows?"

Bilal and I follow Stephanie up a few flights of stairs to a long, narrow hallway lined with office doors. They are small offices, like closets that somehow managed to swallow a desk and a filing cabinet and maybe a folding chair or two. We try to keep up with her around one corner, then another. Up a few stairs, down a few stairs. We walk through a large kind of garage space two stories high, partially open to the outside world. I can see traffic driving up King Street, people going about their normal lives, visiting the grocery or the doctor's office or heading in late for work.

"We're hoping to expand into this space," Stephanie says without stopping. "We're hoping to build some new offices in here."

"That's a good sign," I say.

"Yes, things are going well. The community is really behind us."

She is clearly excited about what it would mean for them, all that extra space, all that extra capacity. In the reception area alone you can hear the hubbub of languages, the urgency of people making a final plea or requesting extended deadlines. I think of the refugees I have met in the community, proud of the jobs they have secured, ecstatic that their children are receiving an education.

The work CWS does is amazing—they greet refugees when they arrive and usher them into their new life with as much support as they can muster. They help them find work, enroll their children in school, and answer any number of questions.

What food goes in the refrigerator?

Where can I buy a sofa?

How do I catch the bus?

Where can I learn English?

Can you help me read my mail?

We walk back inside to a different part of the building. She leads us down a hallway that's also a sort of conference room—on each side of it are a few offices. People come through from time to time. She motions for Bilal and me to sit at a sofa across from two armchairs.

"I'm going to go find Mohammad," she says, leaving the room.

5

If We Are Lucky

October 12, 2012

"He's here," Mohammad said quietly to Moradi. It was hard to believe they were actually doing it—they were actually boarding this small bus with three other families from their village and beginning a long journey, the end of which he could not clearly see.

She stared at him for a moment, and he wasn't sure what else to say. This was it. There was no changing their minds if they got on that bus. They would leave, and in all likelihood, they would never come back. They would never walk through the front door of their home again. They would never again come down that street at the end of a long workday. He would never again reach up and pluck grapes from the small vines that grew along the walls, or go inside the courtyard and walk quietly among the olive trees. They would never again see their neighbors, their extended families. Maybe they would never see their parents again.

His boys would not grow up playing soccer in the same fields where he had played as a kid. Everything would be new. Everything would be a first.

"Okay," his wife said. "Okay." In truth, it had been Moradi who had pushed him to make this decision in the last few weeks. She knew it was the only option for them if their boys were to have any kind of a future.

The six of them bumped through the front door of their home and piled into the waiting vehicle, the boys already sinking under the weight of the packs. Mohammad and his three oldest boys carried the food and water. He wore two backpacks, one on the front and one on the back, like a turtle shell. Moradi carried their toddler, trying to keep him quiet.

On the bus, Mohammad gave the man the money required to drive them to the end of the road, as far south as the road would take them. He thought about the long walk to come, the walk they would have to make as a family later that night.

He looked at his boys. He didn't watch as his house disappeared behind them. He looked forward. To what? He had no particular destination in mind. First, Jordan. That was the only step he knew to take, but he did not have a goal of making it to Europe or Scandinavia or Canada or even the United States. He knew only one thing in that moment—they could no longer stay where they were. Life as he had known it growing up was no more. The war had no end in sight. They had to leave.

He leaned back and ran his fingers through his gray hair, looking around the minibus at the other families. He looked for his boys and counted—one, two, three, four. It would not be the last quick head count. His older three were quiet, pensive, staring out the windows. His youngest was like a small cat that refused to be held, crawling over all of them.

"Easy, easy," he said quietly, pulling the boy close.

They had a long journey ahead, longer than even he knew at the time.

If we are lucky, Mohammad thought, *tomorrow we will be in Jordan. Tomorrow we will begin a new life.*

He paused, not wanting to consider the next thought, but it came anyway.

And if we are unlucky, we will be dead.

6

You Are Friends Now

November 15, 2016

What will this Syrian man be like? I wondered. What will his story be like? Will he feel free to share what he and his family have been through? Will he look at me with scorn? Will he have seen the people on the news who loudly shout they want the refugees to leave and think I am one of those people?

Minutes later, Stephanie returns. Behind her walks a man with graying hair, furtive eyes, and hands that keep folding over on each other—restless hands, nervous hands. He walks slightly hunched, as if trying to remain unnoticed, out of the way. He has kind eyes and looks like he wants to smile but is holding it in check. She introduces us all, and Bilal interprets in the halting way those transactions take place—a word for a word, a phrase for a phrase. He takes extensive notes while Mohammad goes on and on, then relays to me those words, those phrases. When Mohammad smiles, his teeth flash out for only a moment.

I realize he looks older than he is. I would initially have guessed he was in his mid-fifties, but apparently, if my math is right, he is barely forty-five, only a few years older than me. There's a kind of softness in his eyes, as if he has seen so much that he's given up on holding grudges or clutching his anger. His shoulders have a bent-but-not-broken arch, and I see a childlike eagerness to make new friends. I wonder where he acquired his optimism. I wonder how someone 6,000 miles from home can hold so tightly to hope.

I thank him through Bilal (though Mohammad apparently understands some English already) for his willingness to meet me here in a strange country even when he does not know what telling his story might lead to. I thank him for his willingness to explore writing a book with me. I tell him not to get his hopes up.

"Book writing and publishing are no sure thing," I say. "It may very well be that nothing will come of our time together. But I would like to help you tell your story."

Bilal echoes my words to Mohammad in his own language, and Mohammad smiles and nods and answers in Arabic. Bilal smiles and nods again, and turns to me.

"Mohammad says it is impossible for nothing to come of this. He is glad you are willing to hear his story, and no matter what happens, you are friends now. That is all that matters."

The words catch me off guard. I pause, aware of my own breathing. I thought this man would be more skeptical about me. I thought he, a Middle Eastern Muslim, would see me, a white, western Christian, as a potential enemy. But he accepts me without reservation, almost instantly. His quick willingness to befriend me puts me off balance.

Friend. I wonder what he thinks when he says that word, and perhaps for the first time ever, I wonder what the word means to me. Am I a good friend? My life is fairly isolated, dedicated mostly to my wife and children. Do I know what the word *friend* means?

"I'm going to leave you three here to work together, if that's okay," Stephanie says, smiling, clearly happy with the start we've made. I forgot she was there.

I nod. I feel like I'm nodding a lot, like the words aren't there—like I've misplaced all of them and the only tool of communication that remains is for me to move my head up and down on a hinge. I clear my throat and try to rediscover the questions I wanted to ask.

"Mohammad, can you tell me about your village?" I ask him. "Can you tell me about how you got to the United States?"

Bilal relays the question, and Mohammad looks up at me with a sad smile. "I love Syria. No one ever wants to leave their home. But we had no choice."

7

The Long Walk

October 2012

Mohammad's gaze shifted nervously back and forth from the faces of his family to the Syrian countryside flying by outside the small bus. Every seat was taken. There were a number of families from his village who had decided it was time to leave. What would become of them all? How long would these familiar faces surround them? How soon would their paths diverge?

His parents had lived with him and his family—they would be taking over the house. Mohammad tried to imagine them living a solitary life there in the village. He hoped some people would stay if only so that his parents could have some kind of a life. He worried about what they would do if everyone left. His mother probably would have come along with them if it was up to her, but his father was not well enough to travel. He did not like leaving home.

"I would rather die here in Syria than in the wilderness, or in some foreign place," he had told Mohammad. So they remained behind. Moradi's parents would wait for now.

He looked over at his wife where she stared down at their youngest, now asleep, his small brown-haired head bouncing this way and that as the bus rolled along. The boy's name meant "chosen."

For a moment Mohammad felt the thrill of what they were doing, what they were embarking on. He tried to convince himself that in Jordan everything would be made right, his family would find a home, he would find work, the boys would go to school and receive an education. Peace. They would find peace and normal days and neighbors with whom they could drink coffee and talk. The monumental decision to leave everything they owned, everything they knew, would pay off. If not for him, at least for his boys.

Chosen.

The bus dropped off Mohammad and his family in a village in the far south of Syria, as far as the bus would take them, and then Mohammad hired a taxi to drive them to the last village, twenty minutes away. It was as far south as you could go by way of vehicle in Syria. The only thing to do from there was walk. They got out of the cab and stood there with the other families, all of whom had hired drivers to bring them to that place. Everyone stood there for a time as the sky darkened, waiting for who knows what.

Off to the west, the sun set in calm hues of pink and light blue and indigo. The air was completely still. Behind them, Syria—home, family, war. In front of them, Jordan—uncertainty, a long walk.

Hope.

Most of the families they had started off with in the minibus also ended up there in the far south of Syria, and as the sky grew dark and they gathered closer to their family members, they met up with the smuggler, the man who would get them to the Jordanian border. He gave out harsh instructions in a voice like an AK-47. The group fell into a loose formation behind him as he led them away from the lights of the village and into the darkness of the wilderness.

The air smelled of old dust and far-off mountains and their own sweat. Clouds moved in and covered the stars. Mohammad couldn't see anything, but he could hear his boys walking, the food and water jostling in their backpacks. Other children cried or whimpered or begged to be carried.

"Stop!" their leader hissed suddenly. "Get down!"

Everyone in the group dropped to the dust and waited, holding their breath. Mohammad's oldest three boys were quiet and afraid. Their two-year-old breathed softly in his sleep, then woke on the ground and started to cry. Moradi tried to calm him.

"Abba," one of Mohammad's older boys whispered. "Will we be okay?"

"Shh!" Mohammad hissed.

Soon the man leading them stood slowly to his feet. He walked ahead a short distance, disappearing in the shadows. Fear crept in on Mohammad. What if the man left them? What if he took their money and evaporated into the desert? But he came back, crouching, and motioned for everyone to follow him.

"Come," he said. "Quietly." There was the sound of two dozen people rising out of the dirt, gathering their things. There was the rustling of clothing and backpacks and whispered questions.

"Are you okay?"

"Are we almost there?"

"How far do we still have to go?"

And then the sound of people walking, stumbling through the dark, tripping over rocks, cursing, asking where so-and-so was or if a child needed water or if they would arrive at their destination before morning. And always there was shushing.

"Shh! Stop talking!"

There was no path. No road. Only darkness and boulders to climb over and the dust of the desert and ridges that rose in front of them like waves.

Twenty minutes later, the leader stopped. Everyone paused, holding their breath.

"Down!" he shouted again, and they dropped facedown, hugging the dry earth. Mohammad's older boys started crying quietly, their backpacks lying on top of them. The only sounds they made were nearly silent sobs, tremors that turned their mouths down at the corners and shook their chests and made their breath come in halting gasps. But they stayed quiet.

The soldiers came out of nowhere. First there was nothing but the night sky and the boulders and the expanse of dust, and then there were soldiers. They were Jordanian, and they were kind, offering the group water. Each person was registered, loaded into a vehicle, and taken away.

Late at night, or perhaps early in the morning, they arrived at the Za'atari refugee camp, the new home of over 80,000 Syrian refugees. More than half of the residents were children.

In those days, with Syrians coming over the border every day, every night, the refugee camp of Za'atari grew quickly. It became Jordan's fourth largest city. And six of its newest inhabitants were Mohammad, Moradi, and their four boys.

8

Finding Mohammad

December 2016

About a month passes after my first interview with Mohammad. He is busy getting his children settled in school. Thanksgiving comes and goes, a holiday my family always spends in Charlotte, North Carolina. We come back, and winter has arrived. December slides past, icy and cold with lights in the windows. The city is Christmas reds and greens, and our one-year-old is the baby Jesus in our church's Christmas pageant.

We attend a 275-year-old Episcopal church in the heart of Lancaster. The streets are bustling on Christmas Eve. We arrive early, help our children into their costumes, then take our seats along with my extended family. Any child is welcome to join in the Christmas pageant, so the contingent of shepherds and wise men and innkeepers is massive.

My oldest daughter plays the role of Mary, and she walks alongside Joseph. They make the short trek from the back of the church to the front. Everyone chuckles as the multiple wise men, shepherds, angels, and innkeepers assemble at the front. The star also walks to the front, an adorable toddler dressed in a humongous, puffy, five-pointed outfit. One of the young narrators reads a selection from Luke, her voice small and beautiful, her r's sounding like w's. Everyone sits in rapt attention, listening to these ancient words read by a child.

> All returned to their own ancestral towns to register for this census. And because Joseph was a descendant of King David, he had to go to Bethlehem in Judea, David's ancient home. He traveled there from the village of Nazareth in Galilee. He took with him Mary, to whom he was engaged, who was now expecting a child.
>
> Luke 2:3–5

I wonder about that journey for Mary and Joseph, the one that was more than a short walk from the back of the church to the front. They left their home, the people they knew, journeying into an uncertain future. And then later, after Jesus was born, there was the long journey to Egypt:

> After the wise men were gone, an angel of the Lord appeared to Joseph in a dream. "Get up! Flee to Egypt with the child and his mother," the angel said. "Stay there until I tell you to return, because Herod is going to search for the child to kill him."
>
> That night Joseph left for Egypt with the child and Mary, his mother, and they stayed there until Herod's death. This

fulfilled what the Lord had spoken through the prophet: "I called my Son out of Egypt."

Matthew 2:13–15

I try to imagine Mohammad and Moradi leaving their home, walking into the wilderness.

———

I wait to hear back from the publisher about whether or not they want me to write this book about Mohammad. I have many concerns—I worry that I will make myself look like this charitable, overly kind person, someone who sacrifices things to help his poor refugee neighbors. I am not that person, and my refugee neighbors are not helpless.

But the real reason I am hesitant about writing the book is a selfish one, and I tell Maile about it one night while we lie in bed falling asleep after another long day.

"I don't know if I want to write this book," I tell her quietly. "I don't know if I'll even be disappointed if the book doesn't happen."

"Really? Why?"

I pause. "To be honest, I know I'm not a great friend. If I have the choice between hanging out and staying home, you know I choose home almost every time. I don't like it when other people depend on me, because that requires something."

I stop talking, waiting for her to jump in and confirm what I'm saying, but she's silent. I look over at her.

"Mai, I'm scared that if I write this book, it will expose me for the bad friend I am. I'll have to be a good friend to Mohammad, a better friend than I've ever been to anyone else, not only while I'm writing the book but even after I'm finished. That's why I don't know if I should write it. I don't know if I can enter into this kind of commitment."

She turns out the light, and for a moment all I can hear is our breathing.

"Maybe that's why you should write it," she says.

———

January arrives, and writing work is slow, so I start driving even more for Uber and Lyft, trying to make money in the fringe hours when my children are sleeping. I take to the city streets in the early morning, shuttling young adults to college and work. I drive late on weekend nights, safely escorting the intoxicated, listening to long, complicated stories in slurred speech. I get home in the wee hours, slipping quietly into bed so as not to wake my wife. I rise in the morning, bleary-eyed and foggy-brained.

I start driving early on one particular Thursday morning. My brain isn't completely awake, so when the girl asks to go to the subway on Queen Street, I do a double take. Since when does Lancaster have a subway? It dawns on me, as I follow my GPS to the address she entered, that she is talking about the sandwich shop. She seems too young to be opening a business for the day, but there she goes out of the car, taking out her keys, unlocking the door, letting herself in. The morning is still dark, and I know that feeling. In another lifetime, many years ago when we lived in England, I was opening quiet shops before London was fully awake.

I keep driving. Later in the morning, a girl argues with me about the fare being charged to her credit card—even though I don't set the fare and have no way of changing it. Then there is a college kid who graduates this spring and can't decide if he wants to return home to San Francisco or move to New York, where all his friends are headed. There is a quiet, reserved girl who erupts with joy when I put Jason Isbell on the car stereo.

I drive an Indian mother and her son to school. She is so tender with him, commenting on what a nice day it is, asking him if he has everything he needs, reminding him to work hard. She asks me to also drive her home, so I do. She can't believe her school offers Mandarin.

"It's so difficult," she says quietly, expecting no reply from me. "It's so precise."

It's been two months since I've spoken with Mohammad, and in the hubbub of the holidays, I haven't been able to follow up with him. When I finally find the time, I call his cell phone during the day, but it isn't working. I hear the single click of being disconnected. No voicemail, no chance to leave a message. Only a single click.

The only other way I have to contact him is by going to his house, a place I've never been before. I contact someone who knows his address and write it down on a torn-off corner of paper. I stare at it.

Let me tell you this: my preferred method of communication is text or email. A distant second is actually talking on the phone. In third, so far from first you can barely see it, is showing up at the house of someone I hardly know, uninvited and unexpected, and knocking on their door. I can't remember the last time I did this. I can't remember if I ever did this.

But I want to speak with Mohammad again. I want to see him, find out how he's doing, so when one of my fares takes me into the part of the city where he lives, I go to his home. It's nicer than I expected. I thought he might live on one of those abandoned streets, one of the narrow back alleys, or at the termination of a dead end. But his neighborhood is a series of duplexes with yards and tiny driveways behind the houses, all of them flanked by minivans and station wagons. There are wide sidewalks. His house has a front stoop and a nicely painted door.

I sit in my car for an unreasonably long period of time, wondering if he'll remember me, wondering what he'll say. I'm not nervous about ringing the doorbell because he's a refugee—I'm nervous about ringing the doorbell because, once again, I cannot remember the last time I showed up at anyone's house without warning. It offends my twenty-first-century American sensibilities.

Still, I get out of the car and walk up the sidewalk and ring the bell, knock quietly.

One of his sons opens the door—he's perhaps twelve or thirteen years old. Just a guess. He is welcoming and friendly and eager to speak English, the most take-charge kind of kid I've seen in a long time. I wonder if he's this way because, of the entire family, he speaks the best English. I can imagine him taking care of everything for them: talking to the cable guy, going along to the grocery store, asking strangers questions when they are out and about and need to know things.

"Is your father here? I'd like to speak with him," I say hesitantly.

"Come in, come in," he insists, holding the door open firmly in that all-encompassing sort of hospitality displayed by Middle Eastern people.

I go inside and stand there awkwardly, wondering if I should stand or sit, wondering if I should take off my shoes or if that would communicate that I was there to stay. I was not there to stay.

A woman comes into the room—I assume she's Mohammad's wife—and the boy rattles off something to her in Arabic. She hands him her phone and I assume he's calling Mohammad. He presses some buttons and then pushes the phone into my hands.

"Here," he says. "You talk?"

Before I know what's happening, I am holding the phone to my ear. The boy is grinning so broadly he is nearly laughing.

"Hey! Hello!" I say into the phone, disarmed by the situation. The voice on the other end of the line sounds like Mohammad. "How are you? Mohammad? Yes? Can we get together?"

His English has improved a lot. He tells me he has found a job, and he sounds ecstatic about it. No, he can no longer meet during the day. Yes, he would love to hang out again. Perhaps some evening? He gives me his new number. I take my phone out of my pocket and punch it in. I say I'll call in the next few days when he's not working and we'll get together.

"Yes! Please," he says, and I can tell he means it. "Please call. Thank you so much. Thank you."

The entire time I am on the phone with him, his son is motioning with his hands toward the sofa, insisting I take a seat. He beckons toward it like a salesman. *Make yourself comfortable. You don't have to stand here in our home. Take off your shoes.*

"No, thank you," I whisper with a smile, still on the phone. When I finish talking, the boy takes back the phone. When I insist for the tenth time that I must go, he escorts me outside in his socks, grinning the entire time. He walks with me all the way to the curb.

"Thank you," I say.

He nods and gives an embarrassed grin, clearly excited to have had a visitor. I sit in my car and he sprints back to his house, his socks making scratching sounds on the cement.

In that moment he reminds me of my own son, and I'm sorry I didn't stay to talk. I'm sorry I didn't accept his offer to sit on the sofa.

I think of their family the rest of the day while I drive. I'm distracted as I take fare after fare, my mind far from the streets I'm on.

There was the quiet mother. The accommodating son. The father who sounded ecstatic to have landed a menial job with a meager paycheck. They have given me so much to think about.

———

A few days later, I call Mohammad again.

"Is this Mohammad?" I ask.

"Yes! Yes."

"Did you hear about the concert benefitting refugees in the city tomorrow? Do you need a ride?"

It takes us a minute or two of back-and-forth for me to clarify what I'm talking about. There is nothing simple about talking on the phone with someone whose primary language is not your own. My mind spins as I think up simpler synonyms, other phrases that mean the same thing. I try saying the same words more clearly, hoping they will stick. Eventually we understand each other.

"Yes! Yes. Please."

"I'll pick you up around 3:00?"

"Yes. Okay. Thank you!"

9

Finding Hope

January 2017

Once again I pull up outside the small duplex where Mohammad lives on the southwest side of Lancaster. The streets are wide and clean here, the yards well kept. He stands outside on the porch, and when he sees me pull up, he waves and darts back into the house. I park and get out, but before I get to the door of his house he comes back outside with three of his boys.

"Where is your oldest son?" I ask.

"He is with my wife. She is learning how to drive." He laughs and shakes my hand. I can tell he is pleased as well as proud that his wife is learning this, that she is on her way to being more independent.

We herd the three boys into the back of my Suburban. They jump in, giddy at the adventure, crawling over the seats. He shouts stern, fatherly commands in Arabic and manages to get them all sitting in the middle row of seats. I help the youngest put on his seat belt. He laughs at my attempts. He is five or six years old, and he thinks everything is funny.

We drive into the city under a pale blue sky. Mohammad tells me how his job at the dry cleaner is going, how his wife works there now and they each work a long shift, but back-to-back so one of them is home with the boys. Sometimes their shifts overlap, but then only during school hours. He laughs and slaps his leg as he tells me that he received a promotion.

"What?" I ask, wanting to make sure I understand him properly.

"I'm a supervisor now!" he says, as if the entire world has created a simple path just for him, a beautiful path lined with peace and prosperity.

"Well done! Really well done, Mohammad."

"Yes. Now I am making $9.50 an hour."

My heart collapses as I try to imagine supporting my family on $9.50 an hour. I do the math in my head, rounding up to $10 to make it easier. That's $400 a week, plus whatever Moradi can make. So, $1,600 a month.

We both are suddenly quiet, reflective. I wonder what he's thinking, if he's as disappointed in the American dream as I am. Maybe not. Maybe he's simply happy, for now, to have a job.

We park a block away and walk through the cold January day to Tellus360, the venue for Church World Service's refugee concert. The building is three floors plus a rooftop, filled with multiple bars, a restaurant area, and large, open spaces. The main floor often plays host to concerts. It's one of the largest restaurant venues in the city, and when we walk in an hour early, the place is already packed.

I talk with one of the CWS employees, who tells me, "I was going to go pick up Mohammad this afternoon, so I called him, but he said, 'No, I have a friend picking me up.' I said, 'Moham-mad, who is this friend?' I didn't know he had friends."

We both laugh. This is what it means to be a friend in the twenty-first century, I think. As simple and as complicated as that. Do I have it in me? Not only to be a good friend, but to allow Mohammad to be a friend to me? What would my life look like if I made friendship a priority?

———

Soon a line of reporters at the event forms to interview Mo-hammad. Everyone wants to talk to the Syrian refugee, especially in light of the recent executive order, a part of which reads:

> (c) Pursuant to section 212(f) of the INA, 8 U.S.C. 1182(f), I hereby proclaim that the entry of nationals of Syria as refugees is detrimental to the interests of the United States and thus suspend any such entry until such time as I have determined that sufficient changes have been made to the USRAP to ensure that admission of Syrian refugees is con-sistent with the national interest.[1]

Based on the rest of the text of the executive order, it looks like this will be in place for at least the next four months, but most likely longer. Moradi's parents have only just arrived, and it looks like they've made it in under the wire. They are still in the midst of finding a place, getting settled. They brought two of Moradi's siblings with them—one of her brothers and one of her sisters. What a relief it must be, this partial reunification.

I look over at Mohammad. I wonder what he thinks about the order that now keeps his parents in Syria indefinitely, living in his house, the one with the hole in the kitchen wall and the splintered telephone pole outside. Has he heard about it?

But he is smiling and talking and putting his arms around his boys' shoulders. He is chastising his youngest son, telling him to come down off the table. And the reporters shine their lights on him and ask questions and retrieve their sound bites.

Only a few days before, I'd had a conversation with a family member about the travel ban that resulted from the executive order. I felt my heart rate skyrocket. I leaned forward on the kitchen counter, trying not to let my emotions get away from me.

My family member looked confused by my eruption of passion, clearly surprised at my concern. "It's only for 120 days. I don't think it's a big deal. After that, everything will be okay."

I stand now in the midst of the crowd at Tellus360 and watch Mohammad, and I am so proud of him—proud of the way he speaks with confidence, proud of his courage in being there and talking to reporters, proud of how hard he works. It took him years to get here. I look at each of his boys and feel broken, thinking of all the other little boys and girls whose lives are stuck as they wait for a country, any country, to take them in.

There is a gnawing sensation in my gut when I think about how much we're doing in the name of safety. In the name of security. I have a sneaking suspicion there is more to it than that. I look at Mohammad, and I'm happy for him.

During a gap in the interviews, I walk over to see how he's doing. "Everything okay?" I ask him.

"Everything is good. Very good." His eyes shine and I can tell he's pleased that so many people care about Syria. I sit down, and beside him on the table I see a handful of everyday things: a cell phone, a passport, a wallet, a bottle of water. And beside all of those things is a printed piece of paper with a question.

What would you take?

I try to direct Mohammad back to that day. "When you left," I ask, "how did you decide what to take?"

He gives me a wry, sad smile, his classic shy look, and that shrug. Always that shrug. He looks at the table covered in things and shakes his head.

"Seriously, Mohammad," I press him—four years after he rushed his family away from their home, four years after he put backpacks on his boys and wondered if he had put too much in them, if they would be strong enough to carry all that food and water through the wilderness. "What did you take?"

He sighs, as if all four of those years are pressing down on his chest, as if all four of those years have been loaded into a backpack and I'm asking him to carry it again.

"We took nothing," he says.

That is all. *We took nothing.*

He shrugs, and the heaviness of that statement hits me. I try to imagine walking away from everything I have worked for, taking nothing except that which means everything to me: my wife, my children. I try to imagine walking out of my house with only backpacks of food and water. I try to imagine calculating how much my oldest son could carry, my oldest daughter.

How much can an eight-year-old boy carry on a hike through the wilderness?

Who will carry the baby?

I stand back and watch as Mohammad tells his story over and over again, the bright lights shining down. Behind him, through the glass, I can see the city of Lancaster opening up, the streets full of people, the cold winter settling in. It is a world away from Syria.

But it is also his new home. Less than six months in and Mohammad already loves this city, perhaps as much as I do. This, I think, is what people who do not know refugees are missing. How quickly they become loyal to this new place. How quickly they speak of it as their own home.

Tellus360 is so packed I can barely walk from floor to floor. It seems the entire city has shown up to give their support. Volunteers cross paths with refugees they knew from years ago. It is a beautiful thing, seeing so many cultures mingling, so many different races smiling and hugging and welcoming one another. The joy shared between so many cultures is a joy I have never seen or felt before. There is something otherworldly about it.

I see Stephanie from CWS and stop to talk to her for a moment. I go to shake her hand and she laughs.

"Today is not a day for shaking hands," she says, and we hug.

I know she is feeling the same mix of emotions I am. She is heartbroken by the new chaos introduced to their methodical system of relocating people devastated by war; she is scrambling to alleviate the negative effect it is having on families who had, only days before, been so close to arriving, so close to a new life outside of a refugee camp. In the coming days, we learn that CWS may have to lay off some of their employees, at least temporarily. But on this night, everyone is celebrating the love our community is showing. Stephanie is near to tears with gratefulness at the outpouring of support.

"We needed this," she tells me with shining eyes, shouting above the noise of the crowd. I have to lean in close and turn my ear toward her to hear. "This has been in the works for a long time, but the timing couldn't have been better."

I give her another hug and then walk around, enjoying the environment. I chat with people from my church or friends who live in the city or strangers who are wondering where they should go, trying to decide what to see and who to talk to.

I meet my wife and children and mother-in-law downstairs. They are buzzing with the excitement of it all, telling me about the international booths they visited, the people they saw. I tell them how well Mohammad is doing in front of the cameras. Maile smiles. We see friends from the city and talk with them about the amazing turnout. For a moment, as we stand there surrounded by these new neighbors—refugees and old friends alike—it seems that the world is charging forward with love and kindness. It feels like perhaps we could accomplish the impossible.

A few hours later, I go back upstairs, looking for Mohammad. When I find him, he is still surrounded by a crowd. The building has not emptied at all—if anything, more people have flocked to the gathering as the night has progressed.

"I have to leave," I tell him, "but I can come back and pick you up later to give you a ride home. Just call me."

"No," he says. "We are ready. Come, boys."

Abruptly he says good-bye to his friends from CWS, gathers his children around him, and gently nudges his way through the journalists who are still lingering about. I lead them through the crowd—Mohammad's three sons, then Mohammad. I have small children. I know how they can wander off. I keep looking over my shoulder and counting them.

1-2-3.

1-2-3.

1-2-3.

I'm scared I might lose these three little boys in the swarm of so many people. The crowd is loud and boisterous and packed shoulder to shoulder. The stairs are difficult to manage. A band has started playing on the main level and the loud music drowns out any attempts to speak.

We burst out into the cold January evening, and it feels good to be alive in that moment. The sun is going down beyond the western edge of the city, already lost below the buildings. In the east, the sky is a puddle of black ice.

Mohammad claps his hand on my shoulder, and his boys dart around us like butterflies.

"All these people," he says, his eyes shining. "All these people." He clenches his fist and clutches it to his chest. "I feel peace."

———

We drive home quietly through the dusk. In the few short minutes it takes us to drive to his house, the sky is dark. Streetlights wink on. Porch lights illuminate a quiet, lonely street.

I wonder how it feels to be in a new country for six months, to feel the newness and the hope and the fear. When we turn onto his street, does it feel like home?

"Okay," I say, pulling to a stop along the sidewalk. "Well, have a good night. It was great to see you, Mohammad."

I get out and help the boys out of the truck. They plow their way up the sidewalk and race through the cold to their house, shouting at one another, already arguing the way brothers will, pushing and trying to get the edge.

I shake Mohammad's hand in farewell, but he protests.

"No, come in!" he says. "Come in!"

I think of the time. My wife is at home with our six kids, probably very ready for parental backup.

"I should really get home," I say. Again I feel the discomfort of going into the home of someone I don't know well, whose language I don't speak. I don't want to be an inconvenience. I don't want to feel uncomfortable.

"Come!" he says in a voice that clearly states he will not take no for an answer. "Come in. I insist."

I feel like a boy chastened by his parent or a teacher. I don't feel like I actually have a choice in the matter, so I follow him inside and take off my shoes, and we sit on his sofa. The boys are in and out of the kitchen. His wife and oldest son are not home yet. His wife's brother, sister, and parents flow in and out of the rooms. I have trouble keeping everyone straight.

He tells me about his own parents, in their seventies, too old to come to the US.

"When we fled Syria for Jordan, my father told me he would rather die in Syria than travel and die somewhere else." He gives a sad smile and shrugs. "My father is not well enough to travel, not anymore. Besides, no one can come here right now. Maybe someday."

Our conversation jumps from here to there, light and heavy, past and present. He tells me about his recent escapades in buying auto insurance. He went all over the city, visiting insurance offices, and at every one they told him they could not give him insurance until he was here for at least a year. Those who said they would give him a policy quoted him an outrageous price. But he tells me of a woman who heard his story and gave him a normal policy with a good price. He smiles and shakes his head, amazed at the generosity he has encountered in this new place.

He tells me another story, how his new landlord came to him, found out about his life and how hard he was working, and gave him a $200 discount on the rent. Mohammad didn't even ask for it.

"Until I make better money," Mohammad explains. "That's what he said. 'Until you make better money.' He is a good man. He is human."

He cannot possibly know in that moment that this is exactly what I need to hear. I am wearied by the actions of wealthy, powerful men. I find the world an increasingly intolerable place, full of hatred and evil and violence. But then there is Mohammad, reminding me to see the good in the world, reminding me to count our blessings.

He gives me coffee. Again, it's not a question of whether or not I want it—the only question is if I would like sugar. The smooth, black liquid is good. Hours later, I'll still feel it in my veins like a jackhammer. I will lie awake in my bed long after midnight that night, thinking of Mohammad and his family and their humble house in the southern end of the city. I will think of the quiet streets and how happy he is to be a supervisor at a dry-cleaning business.

"I really must go," I say. I put on my shoes, and he walks me out to the car. I see the boys through the window, sneaking the remains of our coffee. My children do that. They are always asking for coffee, and when I say no, they lurk, waiting to gulp down the dregs. Amazing how alike we all are. Amazing how children born 6,000 miles apart will do the exact same things. Amazing how nearly every single human being on this planet wants a quiet place to live, a way to make a living, hope for a future for our children. Peace.

Always the longing and hoping for peace once and for all.

I watch through the window as the boys' grandfather chases them away from the small mugs of coffee, gesticulating wildly with his hands. They scream and scatter, and their grandfather acts as if the greatest treason was attempted and thwarted. I can see his face as he growls at them. I smile. Then I laugh.

"Thank you," I say to Mohammad.

"No, thank you," he says. "It was a good night."

"It *was* a good night."

I get into my car. The streets are dark as I turn around and head back down the hill. I pass him one more time, and he's in his bright white socks on the cold sidewalk, no shoes. I beep the horn, he waves, and for a moment I feel it too.

Hope.

10

Za'atari

October 2012

At two in the morning, an hour after successfully hiking through
the wilderness and into Jordan, Mohammad, Moradi, and their
four boys were ushered into a large white one-room tent. It was
surrounded by a thousand other tents exactly like it, all in rows,
organized into districts. It was cold. There were blankets inside,
folded and in a pile, so they made beds on the tent floor and
tried to sleep.

Later that morning, Mohammad woke up and walked outside.
He was tired from the long day before, but a weight was gone
from him. They had made it out of Syria. They didn't have to
worry about bombs anymore. He walked around, asked questions, tried to find out more about the camp.

Za'atari, while made up of tents, had all the problems, issues,
and challenges that a normal city might have. Accidents happened that required treatment. Pregnant mothers were attended

to and children were born. There was crime and disagreements and misunderstandings. Children needed an education. People, human beings displaced from their homes, wanted to feel a sense of community and hope.

A few times each day, a water truck came around and filled up large water containers spaced one hundred yards apart. Everyone drank from these containers, and they ran out quickly because this water was used for everything—washing, laundry, cooking. It wasn't even good water—it tasted terrible, like baked plastic. Fifteen tents shared a bathroom. There was no electricity in Mohammad's area, so if he wanted to charge a cell phone, he needed to walk a half mile through the camp to a charging station that may or may not have an available outlet. Then he would have to sit there and wait while his phone charged.

Often he hiked to the outskirts of the camp and stood along the chain-link fence, staring out into a wilderness similar to what his family had walked through. The endless tan sand, the rocky outcroppings, the low, pale sky. Where was everyone? Where was the rest of the world? This felt like a foreign planet. It felt like they had been placed in a space shuttle and shipped to a remote spot in the solar system. He lifted his hand and shaded his eyes, trying to see something, anything—a house, a farm, a distant city.

But there was nothing.

Perhaps it's good Mohammad couldn't get a bird's-eye view of where he was standing. A photo taken high above the camp shows an endless mass of tents stretching in rows all the way to the horizon. Mostly white, they're separated by lanes through the dust. It looks like some of them have been pushed together to create larger dwellings. As the sun sets, shining red and orange, small white lights blink on, a constellation of displaced people.

But on the ground and among the tents, it would be easy to believe the rows never ended. It would be easy to believe the world had transformed into this—cities of canvas and plastic—and beyond it, nothing else. Maybe this was the new world. Maybe everyone else had been bombed and sent away, and all that remained were refugee camps encircling the globe.

———

Days passed. Everyone in the camp received a food ration twice a day, brought to each tent by a man in a car. He drove around the camp almost all day, delivering food. After only a few days, that changed to receiving food stamps that came with marks from Saudi Arabia or the Arabian Union. The food stamps allowed them to choose their allotment from a warehouse, which was set up like a grocery store. Mohammad brought the food back and cooked it in a kitchen they shared with eight or nine other families.

During the heat of the day they took refuge in the shade of the tents, and at night they wrapped themselves in blankets and shivered. When the sun was out, everyone stayed inside. They dozed on and off throughout the day, living in that haze of half-sleep. They went for water. They ate dinner, either one that was delivered or one they cooked themselves. They went to bed.

At night, Mohammad lay there, his eyes wide open, staring through the darkness at the white ceiling of the tent. He couldn't sleep anymore. Around him, his boys slept. Moradi tossed and turned. He thought about their life in Syria, the months before they had left. He remembered the sound of the bombs hitting his village, the frantic motorcycle rides to get out of town before the next wave of attacks.

He reminded himself that they had been forced to leave. There had been nothing there for them. At least they were safe in the camp. He could picture the hole in his kitchen wall, the one he had plastered over.

A strong, frozen wind whipped through the camp at night, the tents flapping, the cold air seeping in around the seams. He rolled over, closed his eyes, tried to sleep. When he finally did, he dreamed of bombs falling from the sky and being lost in an endless wilderness.

———

One day their toddler came to the door of their tent screaming, his face covered in blood. His brothers were with him, shushing him, shouting for their parents to come and help. He had been playing with other boys, and someone had hit him on the head with a rock, slicing him open along his eyebrow. Mohammad carried him through the camp, blood dripping onto both of them, all the way to the hospital run by the French. The doctor took a look and put in a few stitches.

Ten days later, they were on their way to the doctor to have the stitches taken out when the boy tripped and cut open his other eyebrow. The doctor patiently removed the stitches from the old cut, now healed, and then put stitches in to close up the new cut.

11

Do You Remember?

January 2017

When Mohammad and I sit on his back patio on sofas he lined up there, and his boys run in and out of the house and ride their bikes along the sidewalk, I will ask his sons, one by one, if they remember the refugee camp.

The youngest boy comes in close and proudly shows me his matching scars, one above each eye. They are the only things he takes with him from that camp, memories passed on to him by his brothers and parents as they retell the story.

The middle two shake their heads and shrug. They were young. They have forgotten the camp.

But Mohammad's oldest sits there with us, often interpreting when we hit a roadblock. I ask him about the camp, what he remembers, if anything.

"It was not good," he says, his normally smiling face suddenly serious. "We needed to leave."

The youngest boy, still staring out at me from under his small scars, laughs, then runs off and hops on his small three-wheel bike, zooming up and down the sidewalk.

I hope he lives to be eighty years old. I hope someday his grandchildren, his great-grandchildren, will reach up and run their tiny, perfect fingers along those scars, those smooth, shining reminders.

Part Two

The Foreigner

It was by faith that Abraham obeyed when God called him to leave home and go to another land that God would give him as his inheritance. He went without knowing where he was going. And even when he reached the land God promised him, he lived there by faith—for he was like a foreigner, living in tents.

Hebrews 11:8–9

12

Neighbors

April 2017

We try to figure out a night when the four of us can get together: Moradi, Mohammad, Maile, and I. Our schedules are tough— their days are full with work and four boys in school, and our evenings are overscheduled, with teenagers' activities and babies who need to be in bed. We finally agree on an evening when our kids are home and can entertain themselves and Moradi isn't working late at the hotel downtown, where she has picked up a job in addition to the one at the dry cleaner.

At first Mohammad says that he and his wife will arrive a little after 7:00. It's Sunday night, and Moradi has to work longer than expected. Later, while he and I are texting back and forth, he says it will be closer to 8:00 before they arrive. Now it's 8:30, and I sit on the porch drinking coffee, wondering if they're still planning to come.

Maile carries things in and out of the house, the front door wide open, the night beautiful. There are small white flowers in the pots that hang from our front porch ceiling, and water drips methodically from the bottom. The city is busy and loud, as it will be for the rest of the spring and through the summer. Every few minutes, someone walks by our house, their eyes down, staring at the cracks in the sidewalk or the phone in their hands. A couple shouts angrily at each other up the street while a loud motorcycle revs its engine, threatening to wake our youngest two children, who are already sleeping.

Mohammad and Moradi pull up in their car, and I walk barefoot down to the sidewalk to help him parallel park into an extremely tight space in front of our house. Mohammad grins at the challenge the whole time, refusing to believe me when I motion that he still has room behind him.

"What?" he exclaims, waving off my insistence. "No!"

Their youngest boy springs from the car like a kid released from school, laughing and giving me a high five. I shout into the house for our eight-year-old son to come out and play, and soon the two of them are kicking a soccer ball back and forth on the uneven sidewalk under the streetlights, chasing it when it gets away from them, shouting for help when it rolls out onto the street.

Mohammad and Moradi come up onto the porch. I shake Mohammad's hand, and he is all smiles. I say hello to Moradi—it takes a deliberate effort on my part not to reach for her hand in greeting or to give her a hug, but I know that, as a Muslim woman, she prefers not to shake hands with men. She smiles and nods hello, and her face is radiant with kindness.

Mohammad told me on the telephone that she did not pass her driver's test, that she was nervous and she cried when the instructor told her she had failed. He said she needs more practice. I don't say anything about the driver's test. I don't want to upset her.

They both look tired. I know they put in long hours, and the weather has been warm. I'm sure a dry cleaner is not the most comfortable place to work as summer approaches. Recently, when I stopped by there to say hello, heat radiated out through the open doors.

I grab everyone a coffee, and Maile brings out some cookies she made. Mohammad and Moradi are both very polite, very quiet at first. Mohammad wears slacks and a button-down shirt that is only buttoned halfway, revealing a white T-shirt underneath.

"It is good to see you, Shawn," he says. "How are you?"

"Good. Very good," I say.

Moradi is dressed in a decorative black robe, fancier than anything I have seen her wear before. It has a zipper up the front lined with tiny, diamond-like jewels. Her head is covered in a black scarf.

Maile talks about how hot it has been.

Moradi nods, eyes wide. "What do you think?" she asks, motioning toward her own clothing with a laugh.

"Yes, you look very warm," Maile says, smiling.

The four of us sit there chatting on that spring night, and I think about what an unlikely group we are.

Maile speaks with Moradi about where she might be able to take English lessons in the fall, and when they run into frequent communication problems, Moradi opens a translation app on her phone. They laugh and point at the word on the screen.

"Yes, 'school,'" Maile says.

"School?" Moradi repeats, and Maile nods.

Meanwhile, Mohammad explains why he would like to move out of the city. "When I was in Syria," he says in short, boisterous sentences, "we knew everyone. All of our . . ." He pauses, gestures around at the other houses.

"Neighbors?" I ask.

"Yes, yes. Neighbors. We knew all of our neighbors. We could send the boys home to a friend's house after school. They could play out there whenever they wanted, without worrying. But here, we know no one. Not even the people who live next door to us. I cannot let the boys go home with friends—we do not know their parents. We know nothing about them. It is hard, living in a city like this."

He takes a deep breath, seeming to ponder the strange nature of a place where you do not even know the people who live next to you. My family has lived in our house for three years and we still know only a handful of people on James Street. I wonder if there are other people like Mohammad on our block, people looking for friendship.

"Out there"—he waves toward some faraway suburban haven—"our boys could run and play outside on their own, instead of always staying in the house. Always. I think it would be good."

I don't have the heart to tell him that the suburbs, at least in my experience, are no more overtly friendly than the city is. That he's living in a country where many people do not know their neighbors very well.

"So," I say, "let's go look at some houses tomorrow."

"Good. Good," he says. "We have our green card appointment tomorrow at 4:00 p.m."

"And you work until 1:00?"

He nods, staring out at where the boys are kicking the soccer ball back and forth. It makes a gritty, skipping sound as it slides along the sidewalk. I can smell a cigarette, the smoke drifting down to us from a neighbor's house.

"I'll pick you up at 1:30," I suggest.

"Okay." He leans back in his chair. He is a man of action—this much I'm learning about him. Once he makes up his mind about something, he does not wait around.

"But now," I say, getting the ladies' attention, "it's time you teach us some Arabic."

We spend the next fifteen or twenty minutes learning how to say "Hello," "Good morning," "Good night," and a host of other basic words and phrases. It's difficult. Really difficult. They make sounds in their everyday speech that I've never tried to make in my entire life. Moradi laughs out loud when I try to pronounce the name of one of their sons.

"Ahmed," I say, making a loud, clearing-of-the-throat sound where the *h* and the *m* come together.

"No," Moradi coaches, grinning. She goes on to make a deeper sound, the kind that comes from down in your throat, closer to your lungs. I try again, and she keeps saying it over and over again. Not this, that. The trouble is, I can't tell the difference between what I'm saying and what she says.

Maile tries to say "Ahmed."

"Yes! That's it!" Moradi says.

"What?" I exclaim. "How is what she said any different from what I said?"

We all laugh. I think about the nature of language—how speaking the language you were born into, and hearing that language spoken to you, feels like going home. Mohammad and his family spend so much time learning English, but has anyone who knows them tried to learn their language? I wonder if any English speakers have stopped and listened and tried to learn their words for *hello, good-bye, good morning.* Their words for *home* or *love* or *melancholy. Homesickness. Refugee. Mortar.*

The boys go inside to play video games. We stop talking and listen to the sounds of the city. Cars go by. In the distance, a siren screams. It's now nearly 10:00.

"Before we go," Mohammad says, "can you help me fill out my green card paperwork?"

"Of course," I say. "Let's go inside, to the table."

The four of us go in and sit there while Mohammad lists off dates and cities and Maile and Moradi talk some more. We have large windows that open out onto the porch where we had been sitting, and the city keeps moving. I hear the kids playing in a neighboring room. I realize the four of us can hang out now, no awkwardness, no sense of strain. We are friends, and we are beginning to understand and recognize the challenges both our families are facing: housing, raising teenagers, making money.

Moradi speaks to Mohammad in Arabic, and he smiles.

"What did she ask?" I say.

"Moradi has another driver's test this week," he says. "I took her to her first test, but she didn't pass. She says I make her nervous."

We all laugh. Moradi playfully imitates Mohammad berating her and we laugh louder. Mohammad clearly understands this is a weakness of his, and he doesn't even try to defend himself. He shrugs and grimaces, then continues.

"She is wondering if Maile"—he stops and points at Maile with something like deference or respect—"can take her for her driver's test this time."

Maile looks at Moradi. "Would you like me to take you to your test?"

Moradi smiles, tilting her head to the side. "Yes. I would. Yes."

We make the arrangements, and I help Mohammad finish filling in his green card information. When they leave, it's late. Maile and I shoo our kids up to bed and take a few minutes to clean up the coffee and the cookie tray. We talk quietly about our new friends, then retreat to bed.

There is something new here, though I can't say exactly what it is—this situation, these feelings. Finding friendship in a place where I first went only to offer a helping hand. Receiving help, perspective, wisdom—all from an unexpected source. Having an almost desperate hope that someone else will make it, will thrive, will find their way. I want for Mohammad the same things I want for my son, for my father, for my friends I grew up with.

Again I find myself thinking in a deeper way about the nature of friendship, this voluntary hitching of your wagon to someone else's.

I pick up Mohammad and we drive to a small town outside of the city, about fifteen minutes north. A friend of mine, a real estate agent, is meeting us at a rental property Mohammad would like to look at. We are still in the early days of searching for a house for them to move to. We're as hopeful as we are naïve.

We park along the street and walk to a house that sits on the corner. There are two apartments here—one upstairs and one downstairs. The Realtor is a friend from my childhood, and he smiles and greets us. I catch up with him on how his mom and brother and wife are doing. He unlocks the door and walks us into the house, then up the stairs to the second floor.

It's basic, nothing special, but nice in its own cozy way. He explains what the rent includes. We talk briefly about the rental application process, and it's the first time I encounter the concept of income requirements.

"There's an income requirement?" I ask, my insides dropping. It has been a long time since I went through a realty to rent a property. I don't know how much Mohammad makes, but I can't imagine it would be enough to give any landlord peace of mind. I was hoping the fact that he had paid his rent on time for the last nine months would be good enough.

My Realtor friend explains that the realty he works for likes to see a monthly income of three to four times the rent.

Meanwhile, Mohammad wanders around the house. "Very nice," he says at each new revelation—another bedroom, a well-organized kitchen, a loft space above the living room. "Very nice."

We go outside. The Realtor explains that he would be responsible for mowing the thin strip of grass between the house and the road. Mohammad nods. We walk up and down the porch and watch the cars go by on the main street.

The Realtor and I shake hands, then Mohammad and I walk back to the car. We sit for a minute before driving away.

"It's nice?" I say, but it's more of a question.

Mohammad nods, shrugs. "I don't like living upstairs."

"You mean the second floor?"

He nods again. "Yes, Shawn. I have boys." He laughs, holding his hands out, palms up. "What can I do? They run around. They are so loud! I would feel bad for someone who lived under us."

I smile. "Good point. So, you're thinking this is a no?"

He shrugs. "I will talk to Moradi. But we should not live upstairs."

We drive back toward the city, my friend and I. For the first time, I'm confronted with a situation so different from my own. If Maile and I decide we want to move, there is very little standing in the way of that decision. I have a long financial track record with good credit. There are so few hurdles in our lives.

For Mohammad, though, moving could cause a major upheaval. With limited income, he has to closely evaluate how the move would impact his travel costs to and from work—could he afford the extra gas if he moves twenty minutes away from work? Because both he and Moradi work, he would need to make sure their new location would conform with his boys' school schedules. Is there a discount grocery close by? Currently his boys can walk to school—how would a move impact that? In the city, he is close to Church World Service and the multitude of services they supply—would a move take him too far from this support network?

We are both quiet on the drive back into town.

13

Falling All Around Us

November 2012

Mohammad was used to living out in the country, surrounded by green space and a big sky. He was used to his daily motorcycle rides on the dirt roads.

He opened his eyes. He was still trapped in a tent city, surrounded by barbed wire, chain link, and a wilderness that held nothing for them. Without thinking, he would often find himself at the edge of the camp, staring out at the wilderness, thinking of the other families who had come from his village.

There were no jobs in the camp. Not all the children could go to school.

In the morning, he woke up, made breakfast, and sat there quietly while his children ate. He looked at Moradi—she was staring at the opening in the tent, the flap dancing quietly in a cold breeze. The sun rose and there was nothing to do. The light coming through the tent door slid across the floor. Ten o'clock.

Eleven o'clock. Noon. They gathered the boys and ate a small lunch. One o'clock. Two o'clock. The afternoon was nothing. The evening came and went. Before he knew it, he was lying in the tent again, the darkness heavy around him.

Sometimes, if he went out at night, he stared up at the sky. The stars were brilliant. The air was crisp and he breathed it in deep, breathed it out in clouds. But day would come again, another day with nothing for him and Moradi to do, nowhere to go, no hope for his children.

He had to leave. He had to find a better life for his family. But the gate was guarded by the Jordanian army, and it was the only way out.

One night they were all in bed, and the wind was so strong that the tent felt like it might lift off the ground. No one could sleep. His youngest son cried out. The other three kept asking if everything was okay. They moved together in the middle of the tent and tried to wait out the storm.

But the wind was getting stronger. Mohammad pried himself out from under his warm covers and scoured the camp for anything heavy to hold down his family's tent. Rocks, cement blocks, anything. He brought the weights he found into the tent and set them in the four corners, but the tent still billowed, still threatened to fly away, so he took the knives they had been given to cook with and used them as extra stakes, pushing them through the canvas and into the rocky ground. Eventually they all fell asleep.

In the morning, Mohammad woke up to find that their tent had collapsed on them. He crawled outside while everyone was still asleep in the flat tent. Many other tents had also fallen down in the wind. Everyone worked together, putting their homes back up. This was when he started asking around to see if there was any way out of the camp.

Mohammad lasted in Za'atari for two weeks. He managed to find someone who would smuggle him out of the camp and into a nearby Jordanian city. They would start over again, this time in a place that wasn't surrounded by chain link, that wasn't drowning in the wilderness.

He had to pay $50 in Jordanian money to escape the camp. They left at night.

14

Learning

April 2017

A few days after our gathering, Maile heads over to the dry cleaner to pick up Moradi from work for her driver's test. She arrives with a lot of time to spare—Moradi would like to drive around a little bit to get used to our car before she has one of those intimidating examiners with her.

Maile arrives at their workplace, which is in a small strip mall west of the city, about ten minutes from our house. She goes inside and looks around. Registers line the front, and the doors are open, letting in cool, fresh air. Mohammad is hanging suit coats on a moveable rack that holds hundreds of articles of clothing going all the way back through the shop. When he sees Maile, he grins and climbs down from the step stool he's on.

"Maile! Hello," he says in his always friendly voice. A young man also comes to the front—Moradi's brother. He arrived from Syria around the same time as Mohammad and his family.

Maile and the two men manage to communicate, exchanging hellos, and then Mohammad goes into the neighboring room to fetch Moradi. She comes out carrying her purse. She has on her covering, pants, and long sleeves with her work shirt over top, baggy, like a smock.

"Hi, Moradi," Maile says.

"Hello," Moradi says. Her voice is quiet, kind, and nervous.

"Are you ready?" Maile asks.

"Okay," she says, shaking her hands in a so-so kind of way.

"Well, we have some time to practice if you'd like."

Moradi nods, and the two women walk out to the car. Mohammad trails along behind. When they get to the car, he pulls some papers out of his back pocket—the paperwork for her appointment.

Maile starts to feel a bit anxious. After all, when is a visit to the DMV ever straightforward? (How many times have she and I gone there with a scheduled appointment only to realize we didn't have the proper paperwork or identification or payment method? One time in particular I went to the DMV, for some reason having only cash on me, only to discover they don't accept cash.)

Mohammad walks Maile through each paper. Then he and Moradi go back and forth in Arabic, seeming to argue for a moment. Moradi is dismissive. Mohammad is insistent. Eventually they stop, and Moradi moves to get into the car. Mohammad waves as they drive away.

"Let's go over to the side parking lot and practice there," Maile suggests. They work on parking and turn signals and drive around the parking lot for a little while.

"Would you like to go out on the road and drive around for a bit?" Maile asks.

Moradi nods, and soon they're cruising the main roads. Suddenly Maile is feeling nervous again. Does Moradi know the rules of the road? She seems to drive rather fast, so Maile points out the speed limit signs and tries to explain what they mean. She points at the signs and then at the speedometer.

"You have to stick to the speed limit," Maile encourages her.

Moradi nods. They continue driving for twenty minutes or so, and the whole time Moradi is taking deep breaths. She doesn't talk much—she's focused on the road. She does say one thing, though, when they stop for a moment at a red light.

"You are a much better teacher than Mohammad," she says haltingly.

"I am?"

"Yes. He talks too much. He makes me nervous." They both laugh.

"You'll do just fine," Maile says.

Later, Moradi pulls up to a stop sign beside a church. "I want to be done," she says suddenly. "Too nervous."

"We're close to the driver's testing place," Maile says.

"Oh, okay."

"Just take a right here, and it's not far away."

Moradi turns right, but then she pulls off onto the shoulder, gets out, and walks around to the passenger side.

"Oh, you'd like me to drive?" Maile asks. "Okay."

They switch spots and Maile drives the rest of the way to the DMV. Moradi is trembling and nervous.

"Are you okay? You don't have to worry. It's going to be okay."

Moradi nods, but she doesn't look like she's convinced.

They arrive nearly an hour early for Moradi's appointment, so Maile asks if she wants to get a drink. They walk together into a sandwich shop full of people, and as they enter, everyone turns and looks. Most people look away, but there's a couple sitting in the corner who are maybe in their sixties. When they see Moradi in her covering, obviously from the Middle East, they glare at her. Maile looks away, embarrassed by them, hoping Moradi won't notice.

The line is long, and they wait for a few minutes.

"Should we go somewhere else?" Maile asks. "This is taking forever."

Moradi shrugs. "I don't need a drink. Maybe good ville?"

"What?" Maile asks.

"Good ville," Moradi says again, slower.

"Oh, Goodwill?" Maile asks. "You want to go shopping?"

Moradi's face brightens. "Yes, Goodwill!"

"Oh, I'm always up for Goodwill," Maile says, laughing.

They walk out of the shop and go a few stores farther up, entering the thrift store. They chat while they look through the racks, sharing about their children, work, school.

Eventually Maile looks at the clock. "We should probably go to the DMV," she says.

Moradi nods, sighing.

They wait in line, and Moradi holds the papers tightly in her hand. At the front of the line, they show the one that has her appointment time. Moradi hands over her identification documents.

"Wait over here," the woman says. "Someone will show you where to go."

A guy comes out of the back room, and Maile's stomach sinks. He is large and imposing, and when he speaks, he's gruff, to the point. Moradi looks more nervous than ever.

Oh no, Maile thinks. Poor Moradi looks like a deer in headlights.

"Get your car and pull around back," he says in a deep, disinterested voice as he walks away.

Moradi looks at Maile, her eyes wide. They walk out to the car and drive it around to the other side of the building.

"That man," Moradi says quietly. "That man." Words escape her as to what exactly she thinks about him. Maile can probably guess.

They sit in the car and watch the man test the girl in front of them—it's a simple five- to ten-minute drive around the large parking lot. Parallel parking is involved, as well as stopping completely, using turn signals, that kind of thing. As the girl slowly makes her way through the test, Maile and Moradi sit together quietly. Maile realizes Moradi is murmuring something under her breath over and over again.

"Are you praying?" Maile asks hesitantly.

Moradi nods. "Yes," she says, her voice trembling.

"I'm praying too," Maile says, and they both laugh nervously. As the girl in front of them finishes her test, Maile shows Moradi the controls again. High beams. Turn signals. Parking brake. It's a cramming session. Maile thinks she might throw up, she's so nervous for Moradi.

The man approaches the car. He seems suddenly softer, and Maile is reassured. "This is going to be okay," she says to Moradi.

Maile gets out of the car and the man takes her place in the passenger seat. After he quizzes Moradi on the various lights and features of the car, they drive off into the parking lot.

Maile sits under a nearby tree and calls me. "She's taking her test! She's driving."

"What?" I ask. "You mean right now?"

"Yes! She's doing it. She's parallel parking," she says, and I can tell she's holding her breath. "Oh! Watch out! Yes! She did it. She did it. That was great. She's doing great."

"Is she nervous? Will she pass?"

"The poor woman is terrified," Maile says. "Wouldn't you be? Oh, watch out!" Maile goes back and forth from talking to me, giving a play-by-play of Moradi's test, to talking to Moradi, who obviously can't hear her. "The man was kind of scary at first. Good job! I don't think I can take our kids to do their tests. This is killing me. That will be up to you. Don't forget your turn signal!"

"How's she doing?"

"She's doing great! I don't want to watch, but I think I should so I can give her feedback. Watch out! She did all the turns. They're coming back! I'll call you later."

She hangs up, and I'm left to wonder what has happened.

Moradi pulls the car to a stop and Maile walks toward her. Moradi opens the door, giving Maile a thumbs-up. She is beaming. The man who administers the test walks slowly around the car toward Maile. He stands there for a moment, filling out the paperwork. Moradi sidles up nervously beside them. For some reason, the examiner chooses to relay the news to Maile.

"Your friend didn't pass the test," he says in a nonchalant voice. "She didn't use her turn signal three out of the four times."

Moradi looks furtively back and forth from Maile to the man, trying to figure out what is going on.

"Oh no!" Maile says. "Are you serious?"

"Yeah, I can't pass her. Tell her to make sure she uses her turn signal." He walks away.

Maile sighs. She turns and looks at Moradi.

"Yes? Yes?" Moradi asks.

Maile shakes her head. "No, I'm sorry."

Moradi looks devastated.

"He said you didn't use your turn signal."

"But I did! I did! That man, no good. Tell him I used my turn signal! You tell him!"

"Oh, Moradi, I can't really do that. He won't listen to me." Maile feels awful. They both climb into the car and drive away in silence.

"I'm sorry," Maile says again. "I thought you did great."

Moradi doesn't reply. She cries quietly.

"Where should I take you?" Maile asks.

"I want to go back to work," Moradi says, staring out the window. Maile starts driving over that way, but then Moradi speaks again. "No, I want to go home."

Maile turns the car around, and they head for Mohammad and Moradi's house. They don't talk the entire time. Maile feels horrible. She wishes she would have paid closer attention. Had Moradi used her turn signal? Our indicator is a little tricky—you have to hold it all the way down for it to stay on, otherwise it only blinks three times. Was it her unfamiliarity with the car that caused the problems?

Maile stops the car along the curb in front of their home, and the two women walk together to the front door. Mohammad must have been watching for them—he opens the door before they even get to it.

"Hi, Mohammad," Maile says.

"Hello," he replies, glancing quickly over at Moradi. She starts talking quickly and abruptly in Arabic. Maile winces as she retells the story. Mohammad looks at Maile for confirmation. She explains what happened, and Moradi interjects from time to time.

"That man, no good!"

"If you want to do your test again sometime, I'm happy to take you," Maile says to Moradi, then turns to Mohammad. "I'm happy to take her."

"I'm not taking that test again," Moradi exclaims.

"She'll take it again," Mohammad says, smiling. He is so supportive and kind to her in her disappointment.

"No, I won't!" she says. She walks past him into the house.

"She'll take it again," he whispers. "Now, come inside."

"I'm sorry, Mohammad," Maile says. "But I have to get home to nurse my baby. She's going to be hungry by now."

He nods. Moradi comes back outside and gives Maile a hug. They both say good-bye, and Maile drives home.

She tells me the whole story on the front porch as our kids are in and out of the house and traffic streams by. We're sad for Moradi. I know how much they both would like the freedom of having their driver's license, and I know Moradi would feel more at home if she had the independence of driving. It puts us in a sad state of mind—I'm sure it's even worse at Mohammad and Moradi's house.

I smile, though, when Maile tells me about Mohammad's gentle reception of the news. He has none of the cartoonish anger Arabic men are so often portrayed as having. He is not stern with his wife in any way, and Maile says there was no disappointment *in* her—only disappointment *for* her. He is a good husband.

I'm learning so much from him.

15

The Unexpected Guest (or, My First Ramadan Meal)

June 2017

In Lancaster, early June days are full of hope. Spring has worked her magic to completion, the long green summer is upon us, and the heat starts descending in visible waves. Children run down the city sidewalks, shouting, sensing the end of school just around the corner.

I drive for Uber and Lyft less often in the summer. Lancaster is, among other things, a college town, and the demand for rides goes down when the students head home and teachers looking for summer work decide to drive. But there are still some nights when I go out, drive the streets, listen to people's stories.

Mohammad calls me in between fares and we chat for a few minutes. Every time we talk, he invites me over.

"Come by my house tonight," he says. "Anytime after 8:00."

I tell him I'll do my best, and when one of my fares takes me into his neck of the woods around 8:30, I turn off my driving apps and head for his house. The street is dark and quiet. The sun has only recently set. When I get out of the car, I can hear children playing a few streets over. Someone launches a solitary firework off in the distance. It peals into the black sky, a streak of white, and explodes in a single shot.

I ring the doorbell and can hear it echo inside the house. It sounds far away. Everything seems quiet. Mohammad's house is a pinpoint of quiet in the teeming mass of our small city. I knock quietly, tentatively, on the window beside the front door. The narrow blinds bend upward as some small person peeks through to see who is ringing their bell so late. Tiny fingers push the blinds apart. Eyes sparkle and dance, and I see a smile.

The blinds collapse back together and I hear one of Mohammad's four boys shout something in Arabic. Everything in Arabic sounds urgent to me. Every time I hear someone speaking in that language, I think they're arguing or stating their case or passionately imploring for an idea that could save the world. But when Mohammad's family speaks Arabic and I ask them what they're saying, more often than not it's something simple like, "He wants to go outside" or "He wonders where the closest swimming pool is."

The door opens, and Mohammad stands there in a white undershirt, loose jeans, and bare feet. He gives a wide smile, and I can see why he called me earlier in the week about finding a dentist who would accept his insurance. There is a new gap along his bottom row of teeth, perhaps six or seven teeth wide.

"Your teeth!" I say.

He still smiles, seemingly unaffected. "My, um, how do you say it? Broke."

"Was it a bridge?"

"Yes, that's it. A bridge. It broke." He shrugs. That seems to be his universal reply to whatever life hands him. "What can I do?" he sometimes says with the shrug. The more I get to know him, the more I think this is not a terrible way to view the world. I don't know if I've ever heard him blame anyone for the things that happen to him. He just shrugs.

We shake hands, and he welcomes me into the house. I can tell they're eating. I have dropped by in the middle of a meal, and immediately I feel guilty.

"Did I interrupt your dinner?" I ask.

"No, no, no. Come in. Come in."

Moradi comes around the corner from the dining room and welcomes me with her kind, quiet eyes. She bows her head slightly, respectfully, and her words are always so gentle.

"Come," she says. "Eat."

Their four boys also have come into the living room to see who has arrived, and they follow me into the dining room like puppies, bouncing around and smiling up at me. Their oldest son leads the way, and when we arrive in the dining room, when I see the feast spread out on a plastic mat on the floor and hear Muslim prayers coming through the cell phone set up on the counter, I realize something.

Of course, I think. *It's Ramadan*. Is this why he invited me over after 8:00, after the sun set—so I could eat with them?

The main practice during Ramadan seems to be fasting, and Muslims do not eat or drink anything while the sun shines. Fasting is one of the Five Pillars of Islam. Being hungry redirects a

Muslim's mind so they consider the suffering of the poor, practice self-control, and cleanse their body and mind.[2]

Mohammad's family is one week into their month of fasting from food and water during daylight hours. Because the sun has been rising so early, they did not eat breakfast that morning, so this is their first meal of the day. Everything smells amazing. There is some kind of spinach and potato dish, a salad with greens and cream, a slightly spicy beef dish, and the large flatbread they eat at every meal, including breakfast. The boys drink orange soda in red Solo cups, a drink they savor, sipping it quietly. It's clearly a treat.

"Sit, sit," Mohammad insists, beckoning toward a space on the floor at the edge of the plastic mat. It's been vacated by his son, who now stands in the kitchen, drinking his orange soda and smiling.

Moradi fills a plate for me with more food than I think is possible to eat. She mounds the food into a delicious-looking serving and hands it to me. I sit at the edge of the plastic, cross-legged, leaning over the plate. I am not very flexible.

We eat mostly with our hands, mopping up the delicious juices with the bread. I use a spoon they give me. The boys have already finished eating, but they wait patiently for the adults to finish. The prayers continue on the phone, a wavering voice Mohammad and Moradi listen to quietly. The dark sky peeks in through the windows, and their kitchen light is turned off so that the dining room sits in restful shadows. Everything feels peaceful.

The prayers come to an end on the phone. We talk about work and how school is going. We try to creatively communicate words like "lamb" and "six-cylinder" and "dental insurance." Each time we make a successful connection, we laugh and smile as if we have just learned each other's language in its entirety. Then we stumble through another sentence, another conversation. Communicating with each other is a determined act, a kind of fighting against the darkness.

Some of my family members are terrified of Muslims. They glean from the news the worst of the world and project it on everyone who bears that label. I wish they could be there with me in the quiet, in the half-light. I wish they could eat this food and see this family, their devotion, their kindness, their hospitality. There is something here in this meal, some measure of beauty, that I have rarely experienced with others.

One of the boys says something in Arabic and the others laugh, and I can tell they're laughing at me. I smile and shift awkwardly on the floor.

"Okay," I say to Mohammad, "what's so funny?"

"You're not used to sitting like that?" he asks with a small grin. I realize I've been shifting my position every few minutes, trying to get comfortable. I laugh. The way they sit—it's cross-legged but also different, somehow forward so that their feet are tucked up under them. I saw men sitting like this in Turkey.

The boys laugh unreservedly now, and I laugh with them. "No! I can't sit like this. What happened to your table?"

"We had it for a few weeks. But we did not like eating at a table, so I took it apart and got rid of it." Mohammad makes a tossing gesture toward the door.

"This is how you eat in Syria?" I ask. "On the floor?"

"This is how we eat in Syria," he replies, nodding and taking another large bite.

I take another bite too, savoring the delicious food, so foreign, so good. I can only imagine how amazing it would taste after an entire day of fasting from food and water. I'm impressed by their devotion, their determination. A month is a long time. Mohammad already looks like he has lost weight, and only one week has passed.

"Do you miss Syria?" I ask him, and he nods.

He starts to speak, then stops, his eyes welling up with emotion. He clears his throat.

"The boys," Moradi says. "They miss Mohammad's mother especially."

"Their grandmother?" I ask.

She nods. Clearly it is the first time she has heard the word *grandmother*, and she uses it immediately, trying to familiarize herself with it. Again I am reminded of how difficult it is to learn a language, how hard it is to adopt a new way of speaking.

"Grandmother. Yes, their grandmother. But they are able to Skype each week. They tell her about school, about living here. They miss her."

We finish eating and Mohammad invites me onto the back porch. We sit on the couches he has arranged under a small awning. He takes out a cigarette and inhales a long draw, sighing out the smoke.

"Don't you get thirsty working in the heat at the dry cleaner all day?" I ask him.

"It is hot," he admits. "But we do our best. If you must drink, you must drink, and it is okay. But if you break the fast by eating or drinking during the day, you give a gift to charity, since you were not able to keep the fast."

"So, you can drink if you need to, but you have to pay for it?"

He nods. "I have not had to drink water yet, but the weather has been cool. We will see. I have friends who live in Norway, and the sun does not set until midnight or later! I don't know how they do it. They have to eat a big breakfast before they go to work, because the days are so long there."

He tells me about a new job he is trying out, driving for an egg company on the weekends. He asks my opinion on purchasing a more fuel-efficient vehicle. I explain to him the best way to find a dentist through his insurance. I tell him he might not have dental coverage, but I'll help him make some calls next week during the day.

Moradi comes out carrying three tiny mugs of strong coffee much like espresso. The coffee is the color of dark chocolate, and she serves it piping hot with lots of sugar. It reminds me of the coffee I had in Istanbul when I traveled there a few years ago.

The boys come pouring out of the house through the back door, and the youngest pulls his Big Wheel from the shed and rides it on the sidewalk. A neighbor boy joins him, and they fly up and down the sidewalk in the dark, their wheels rasping, their voices calling out to each other, alternating between Arabic and English.

There it is again, that tangible sense of hope. Could there come a day when we could live alongside each other in peace, speaking whatever language it is that we speak, sharing stories, eating our different foods together?

Their youngest son pedals faster, his tiny legs pumping. A car approaches, and Mohammad shouts a warning at the boy, who pulls into the grass while the headlights pass. Then he's back at it, riding back and forth at breakneck speed.

"I would still like to find a place outside the city," Mohammad says. "I'd like to have a place with some land, a place I can have a garden, grow potatoes and carrots and . . . what is it called? Corn? Yes. Corn."

The night grows deeper and the city settles into it. The stars try to break through the light pollution. Someone lets off fireworks again, far away.

"I really have to go," I say, finishing my coffee. "I have a lot more driving to do tonight."

"No!" Mohammad exclaims as if I've told him I'm dying. "No! Shawn, stay." He insists that I stay, and he beckons toward the sofa I have just stood up from, but I only smile and thank them for dinner. They promise to have our entire family over sometime soon. I tell them they don't know what they're wishing on themselves, and they laugh.

I walk around the side of the house, back to my car. The youngest boy and his buddy are still riding on the sidewalk, laughing and crashing into each other. The boy shouts something in Arabic, then in English. The other boy laughs as if it's the funniest thing he has ever heard, and they're off again, riding through the darkness.

Every time I leave Mohammad and his family, I feel I've been given so much. Every time I leave them, I feel they have given me a small gift of peace, a kind of shalom absent from so much of our culture these days.

It's good to have friends who live quiet, peaceful lives. It seems strange to me that of all the families I know, most of whom are Christian, Mohammad's family lives the most quiet, peaceful life of all.

16

Deeper into Jordan

November 2012

The man they paid to smuggle them out of the Za'atari refugee camp took them in the middle of the night to Ajloun, a city thirty miles or so to the south. Deeper into Jordan. Farther from Syria. There was no turning back now—each journey, each decision, took them down a road toward a new life. What kind of life that might be, Mohammad still had no idea.

Everyone was half asleep when they arrived at Moradi's uncle's home. He had left Syria a few weeks before Mohammad and had managed to get a small apartment. There wasn't nearly enough room for six other people, but they could stay there for a few nights sleeping on the floor until Mohammad could find a place for his family to live.

Those were long, quiet nights, and again Mohammad found himself staring up at the ceiling while everyone lay around him, sleeping or stirring, deep in their dreams. How would he take care of his family in this country, where he was not allowed to work due to his refugee status, where his children could not attend school unless they paid exorbitant amounts of money? But he brought himself back to the present—the first hurdle was to find a home. He would worry about everything else after that.

During the day, he walked the city streets, avoiding the gazes of Jordanians who were tired of Syrian refugees, tired of them taking their menial and black-market jobs, tired of seeing them in the news. By 2016, Jordan was home to over 1.4 million Syrians, 600,000 of whom were registered refugees. And while Jordan had promised its citizens it would create five jobs for every Syrian it employed, that eventually began to feel like an empty promise.[3]

When Mohammad finally found an apartment in the city, he was ecstatic. Maybe this was it. Maybe this was a place they could put down roots, where he could find work and figure out how to get the boys into school. He came to an agreement with the landlord and paid for the first month's rent, money he was able to pool together from his uncle and his brother, who lived in the UAE.

On the second of the month, the day after they came to an agreement, the landlord came looking for him. Mohammad was outside, while inside the house, Moradi and the boys were getting settled, getting used to their new place, making a list of things they needed.

"Mohammad," his new landlord said, "you have to leave."

"What are you talking about?" Mohammad asked. "You said you would rent this house to me."

"You have to leave. I need my home."

"No!" Mohammad said, but then he thought about his precarious position. He was a foreigner in a Jordanian city. He tried to compose himself. "You have to give me time," he pleaded. "I have a wife, four children. You have to give me at least a month or two to find another place! I cannot find a home now. Not today. Not in one day."

The man stared at him for a moment. "I will give you one week."

"I cannot find a home in one week!" Mohammad said. "I want to live here."

The man turned and walked away. He would never return the month's rent Mohammad had paid.

Mohammad walked the streets of Ajloun, so angry he trembled. When he thought of his wife and boys, how excited they had been to move into that apartment, he thought he might cry right there on the street. He didn't know what to do.

A friend called him at this moment, a Jordanian friend he had made who drove taxi in Ajloun and the surrounding cities.

"Mohammad," he said, "where are you?"

"I'm walking. I'm walking, and I'm angry."

"Why? What's wrong? Why are you angry?"

"Do you really want to know?" Mohammad asked. "Okay. Fine. My landlord has said we must move out, even though I just paid him for the first month yesterday. My family is going to be very sad."

He paused, gathering himself. People walked by him on the sidewalk. Cars moved along slowly, honking their horns, idling at the intersections.

"I don't know what to do," Mohammad said. "I don't know where to go. I want to take my family and leave today—I cannot bear to stay for one more week in this man's house. I have to take my family away. I don't know what he might do, maybe something even worse. This is not my land. This is not my country."

Mohammad paused again, but his friend didn't say anything, so he continued. "This is not my country! I don't know the law! I don't even want to be here! I don't know anything. I'm scared to stay in this man's house."

"Mohammad, listen. Where are you?"

Mohammad explained where he was.

"I'm coming now," his friend said. "I'm coming to get you. Just wait there. Don't go anywhere."

When his friend arrived, Mohammad again explained what had happened. He got into his friend's car, and the man drove around while they talked.

"I don't have a home," Mohammad said. "I don't know what to do. I don't know what to tell Moradi."

"I don't know anyone here in Ajloun who has a home," his friend said, "but I have an idea. My sister has a home outside the city, in the country. It is small—tiny, really. It has just one bedroom, one main room, and one bathroom."

"Can I see it?" Mohammad asked.

They drove outside the city, and Mohammad told his friend all they had been through. So many things had happened already. Mohammad didn't know what to think. The man drove him out away from the busy streets, to where the houses were spaced far apart. They pulled up to a small bunch of houses grouped together, and his friend showed Mohammad the small house.

"That's okay with me," Mohammad said after taking a look around. "We can do something out here. We can live here."

———

Mohammad went back and told his family what was going on. As Moradi listened, her face grew closed. Mohammad knew she wanted to go find that landlord and tell him what she really thought, but she didn't say this, and besides, they both knew there was no point. She took a deep breath, nodded, and walked away.

By the end of the day they had gathered their meager belongings and moved into his friend's sister's home. Mohammad's mother even came from Syria to visit them, staying with them for four months. They all lived there in that house, together. Their youngest slept with them in the bedroom, and sometimes the other boys slept there too. They ate together on the floor in the main room. Mohammad cooked. Moradi cleaned and stood at the door, looking with empty eyes at a country that still didn't feel like home.

———

Eventually Mohammad and his family had to move out of that house, and during the next year or so, they moved from place to place, always staying close to Ajloun. Someone else Mohammad knew, someone who lived in a city called Irbid, called him.

"Why do you live in Ajloun?" this person asked him. "There is more happening in Irbid. You should move here."

"I only know one person who lives there," Mohammad said, "and that person is you."

"Come, come. See if you like it."

Mohammad was not allowed to drive in Jordan, so they had to take a bus everywhere they went. He visited Irbid and liked it, so after their first year in Jordan, spent mostly in Ajloun, they moved to Irbid. The war in Syria was intensifying. Mohammad watched the news, shaking his head, wondering when it would all come to an end.

———

Once Mohammad and his family moved to Irbid, he registered as a refugee and received 175 Jordanian dinar from the UN every month for his entire family. Rent alone was 100 to 145 dinar per month, but what were they to do? During their final year there, the UN also gave a sort of monthly food allotment to each family: 20 dinar per person. It was subsistence living, and they went from month to month, searching for cheap food, moving to another apartment—always another apartment.

There was no other plan, no other place than Jordan. Mohammad had family who had successfully immigrated to places like Scandinavia and Canada. He even had a cousin and a sister in the United States. But those avenues were tightening. By 2016, there were over six million Syrian refugees alone, and most countries' intake valves were clogged by a slow, methodical process.

There was nothing else.

Their apartment was like a prison. They rarely left. The boys were not in school, so Moradi taught them what she could. Mohammad was still not allowed to work, so he stared out the window or wandered the streets of Irbid, trying to figure out how to improve their life. Where could they go? What could he do to make money?

No matter where they lived, Mohammad took his walks. He wandered out the front door of whatever apartment or house or row home they lived in, searching. For what, he didn't know. He rarely left on a particular mission, but for him, walking meant moving. Walking meant hoping. But his walks in Jordan started to feel like walking in circles. He would reach the edge of whatever town they lived in and stare out at the wilderness. Always the wilderness.

He had escaped the refugee camp, but he was starting to get the same feeling again, the sense that he was living at a dead end.

Occasionally Mohammad would have to travel to the UN office to fill out paperwork or ask questions about the benefits they were receiving. During his trips there, he sometimes heard rumors about a program that was sending Syrian refugees to the United States. His heart leaped at the thought of moving to the US, but this surge of hope was always followed by a deep sense of skepticism.

That could never happen, he told himself. *There are too many refugees. Too many people wanting to go to the United States. More than a million people, and how many can they take? Five thousand? Ten thousand? Twenty thousand? Maybe not even that many? Probably not me. Probably not my family.*

But people he knew were making progress. People he knew were leaving. One of the first of his friends who had left took his family to Finland. Other Syrians he knew were heading to Canada. He started going to the UN office every week, asking about these programs, but he could never make any progress.

When he went home, he told Moradi, "I haven't gotten a call yet." He looked away from her eyes that were hungry for good news and shook his head. "This is not for us. This will not happen for us."

The days blended together. Wake up. Drink coffee. Try to figure out how to get the kids outside somewhere for a few hours. Sit in the apartment. Eat a small lunch. Sit in the apartment.

Wait for dinnertime. Eat. Sit in the apartment while the sun sets. Go to bed.

But always, during the day when the walls closed in around him, he escaped, walking the city. He walked the streets and wondered what would become of his family. They couldn't go on like this forever. They would have to leave Jordan eventually.

One day while he walked, his phone rang, and he didn't recognize the number. "Hello?"

It was a girl on the other end of the line. "Mohammad?" she asked.

"Yes, who is this?"

"I'm calling from the UN," she said. "Do you want to move outside of Jordan?"

"Outside of Jordan?" he asked. "Where?"

"I don't know yet. But is that what you're hoping for? Is that what you would like? To live somewhere else?"

"Yes, yes. What do I need to do?"

"Okay," she said. "Thank you. We'll call you if something develops."

That was it. Mohammad didn't hear another word for six months. And so he walked the city. Moradi taught the boys as much as she could. Together they waited.

17

A Place He Will Not
See Again

September 2017

I sit in the dim light on our front porch, waiting for Mohammad.
The night is cool, and the people walking by wear sweatshirts or
light jackets. A car with a loud muffler roars through the traffic
light. I take a sip of coffee. I wait, enjoying the relative quiet.

A breeze sweeps down James Street, rustling the leaves in the
monstrous sycamore that grows in front of our house. The large
lower branches are themselves the size of trees, and I consider
the complex ecosystem of the tree, how it stays alive here in the
middle of all this asphalt. Somehow it manages to reach below the
hard surface it's surrounded by, down, down into what might still
be rich soil. I once heard someone say the soil here in Lancaster
is among the richest in the world. How quick we are to cover
over the things that hold such rich benefits.

The skin of a sycamore, especially one this old, is always peeling. The thousands of leaves make a hushing sound as if secrets are being told. It's one of the oldest species of trees on earth, and it's nice to imagine that it might know something I do not, that it has seen more than I have.

Mohammad arrives in his old Mitsubishi, and I move my car to make a parking space for him on the side of the street. He waves, grinning, but when he gets out of his car, he looks weary. He stretches and yawns. He is wearing jogging pants and a button-up, long-sleeved shirt, mostly unbuttoned. Again I think about the long hours he works.

We shake hands. His smile is boyish, and for a moment I can see him thirty years ago, a teenager with lots of energy, ready to embark on his life. I can see his sons there in that smile.

"How are you, my friend?" I ask him.

"Good, Shawn. Good." He is always good. I wonder what terrible circumstances it would take for him to answer with anything else. We walk up onto the porch.

"Inside or outside?" I ask. "It's a little cool tonight."

"Outside, outside," he says in a singsong voice. "This weather. So good."

I agree with him. Fall is my favorite season. I'm always happy to see summer go. A cool breeze races down James Street, and the sycamore is alive again.

"Coffee?" I ask.

"Yes, yes, please."

I walk into the house to make coffee, and his thanks follow me inside. My children are all up in their rooms now, asleep or reading. This is the quiet hour, when Maile and I can usually be found cleaning up after a long day, or in bed, reading.

It feels like we have so few free hours these days, which means we are deliberate with our time. I wish I had more free time for Mohammad. I wish our lives intertwined more naturally than they currently do.

I take him his cup of coffee, black, but I know he won't drink all of it. I think the normal cup of American coffee is too weak for him—certainly if the coffee he normally gives me at his house is the standard. I have to figure out how to make that Turkish espresso Moradi gives me, the stuff that keeps me up through the night. He would like it if I surprised him with a small mug of that coffee during one of his visits.

We sit quietly for a bit. This is something he is teaching me—a willingness to sit quietly with my friends, a willingness to let time pass without feeling an urgency to fill it with noise.

"We have mountains in Syria," he says. "Did you know that? These mountains, they have snow on top."

I wonder where this thought comes from. He rarely brings up his home country without me digging for information. It seems odd, his reflective melancholy.

"Really?" I ask. "I didn't know that."

"Yes, very big. Very big."

We sit there in silence for a bit longer, listening to the traffic, watching the moon rise above the buildings across the street. It's a quiet night for the city, but that does not mean it's quiet. There is always the sound of tires on asphalt, always the sound of someone shouting at someone else. Even the light seems to carry noise along with it, a barely discernible hum that surrounds us, as common as the oxygen in the air. We contemplate snow-capped mountains 6,000 miles away, rising above a land torn apart by war. I wonder what the view of Syria would be from the top of those mountains. I wonder if you could see the bombs exploding, or if, from that high up, all would be peace and calm and the beauty of the wilderness.

"Do you ever miss Syria?" I ask him. "Is there anything you miss?"

I ask him this probably every time we are together, or maybe every other. I don't know why. It's one of the questions that always comes to mind, maybe because of how important place is to me, how rooted I feel to this county, this part of the world.

When I drive down the back roads lined with cornfields, out in the area where I grew up, it transports me to a simpler time. East of the city, I know every road. In the square miles around the farm where I grew up, I recognize every field, every curve in the Pequea Creek. I mined those parking lots for fool's gold when I was a child, chipping away at the asphalt with a penny. I fished along the banks of the creek. Maybe that's where I first encountered this silence that Mohammad is reintroducing me to. Maybe that's where I learned to sit and wait.

As I think about the places where I grew up, I wonder about Mohammad and the settings that made up his childhood. Will he ever experience that again in his life—the feeling you get when you drive down roads that remind you of your childhood?

Normally when I ask him if he ever misses Syria, he laughs as if it's the silliest thing he's ever heard. Normally he exclaims his love for his new country, the perils of war in the old, and the opportunities that await his sons here, where they can receive an education, where there is hope.

But tonight something is different. He is like an old sycamore with roots that reach far below the visible surface of the city for some deep well of water, for something it cannot quite grasp.

"Yes," he says in an almost mournful voice. "Today, yes. Today I miss Syria. Today is Eid. In Syria, today is a holiday."

"Oh, yes," I say. I'd heard something about it on the radio earlier that day. "It's a festival, right? A celebration?"

"Eid is about Abraham. We have four days off, a long weekend. Today would have been the first day. There is no sleeping on these days—we go to market or we spend the day shopping or eating. We meet with everyone. Everyone!" He laughs, but it's a sad laugh, as though he's almost unable to believe how far away he is from Eid, how far away his life has taken him from all the familiar things.

"Your family and friends?" I ask. "Is that who you would have spent the day with?"

"Yes!" he says, and there is a longing in his voice. "All the people! This day, after the morning prayer, we go to the . . . I don't know the word." He waves his hand, thinking hard.

"The mosque?"

"No, no."

"The Hajj? Are you talking about that?"

"No," he says, his voice suddenly gruff, seeming frustrated that the words are so difficult for him to find. "That is Saudi Arabia. No. On the morning of the first day, we wake up early, go to prayer, and after that . . ." He pulls out his phone and types a few words into his translation app. He shows me the screen.

"Oh, the tomb? The cemetery?"

"Yes! Yes. The tomb." He says *tomb* with a hard *t* sound, almost a *d*. "We go to the cemetery. We go there on this day to see our families' graves. We visit the graves of people who have died. Our relatives who have died. Even today, my friends send me photos of them in Dara'a, visiting the tombs."

He shows me a photo. There is a man his age sitting among the gravestones, and beside him are two children. They look like they're praying. Their faces are sincere, reflective. Sad. The ground is a light-colored dirt that looks hard and hot.

"There we read the Koran. You know?"

I nod and take a sip of coffee. He breathes in his cigarette.

"And this is the memorial of Abraham offering his son Isaac, right?" I ask.

"Yes." He nods, watching the traffic. "Yes."

"That's a common story among Islam, Christianity, and Judaism. All three tell the story of Abraham offering up his son."

He is quiet again. I can tell it has been heavy on his mind, not being home for this holiday. I remember the years my wife and I lived in England, how difficult it was to be away for Thanksgiving. We would hold our own celebration in our tiny cottage on the Saturday of Thanksgiving, since we wanted to invite friends over but they did not have work off on Thursday. We crammed everyone we could into our small dining room, the fireplace roaring. We had to cook the turkey in our landlord's oven since it didn't fit in our own small oven. We drove back and forth all morning, taking food to their house to be cooked and then bringing it back.

But no matter how hard we tried, it never felt the same. Holidays abroad are fun, but without our friends and family in the States, they feel empty, like play-acting.

"How is your wife?" I ask. "How is Moradi?"

"Good, good," he says, still clearly distracted by Eid in Syria, by the thought of tall, snow-capped mountains. "She did not come tonight because we were very tired. We got off work late. It was a long day."

As the night progresses, the silences between us become longer. They are not uncomfortable. Sitting in the city means there is always something to listen to. And we are both tired. Our lives race along, only occasionally able to cross. He coughs.

"Did you have any luck finding a dentist?" I ask. Insurance has not been helpful. Most dentists are saying the work on his teeth will cost $6,000 or $7,000, money he clearly does not have. Who does have the money for medical care these days? Most of my friends don't go to the doctor or the dentist anymore unless the issue is life-threatening.

"I spoke with CWS today," he says. "I told them I need insurance that covers dental. We will see." He shrugs.

"Insurance here is hard. Complicated."

"You know, I can go to Jordan right now and pay $1,000 for this work. To do it here, it is over $7,000. That's not good! In Syria, maybe $500, maybe $600. Not now, but before the war. Then, everything was very cheap. Very good. Before the war, everyone came to Syria for this kind of work." He laughs, finding it hard to imagine how much his own country has changed.

A group of teenagers walks by, laughing and shouting.

"When did the war begin?" I ask. "When did things change for you?"

He pauses for a moment. "In 2011, I think."

"Where did you live?"

"In my village. But it started in Dara'a city. After that, it went to a neighboring village, a small city. After that . . ." He shrugs, indicating everywhere.

"Do you think this war will end soon?"

"I hope. I don't know. I hope it's done soon. We need peace. I heard a man from Jordan talking this morning, and he said,

'Everyone in Syria is tired. Everyone is done. We just need peace. Seven years is too long. No one cares anymore what peace will cost them—they only want peace.' Now, I cannot see my mom, my dad, my brothers, my sisters. I will never see them, maybe never again."

I recall the photo of the man and his children sitting beside the grave, performing the traditions of Eid.

"Do you have relatives who died in the war?"

"Yes," he says, and his voice is haggard. Heavy. The weariness is settling in, deep.

We sit quietly.

"It's been over a year now since you arrived," I say.

"One year, one month, and nineteen days," he replies, smiling.

"What do you think of it so far? How is it?"

"You know, Shawn, I like it here. You know why? I live here in peace. I don't see any problems. I live with my wife and children, and I am here for my children. I am old now—forty-six. But my kids are small. They are young. Maybe they can learn here, in this peace. Maybe in the future they can become doctors, teachers. I hope so." He pauses and shrugs again. "What can you do?"

"What time do you work tomorrow?" I ask.

"Eight. I start at eight, but I don't know what time we'll finish tomorrow night. We have a lot of cleaning to do tomorrow for an inspection at the dry cleaner. Someone is coming."

The night, in its slow progression, has become almost cold. He stands up and stretches again.

"I should go," he says. We shake hands.

"Thank you, Shawn."

"Thanks for coming over, Mohammad."

He walks down the porch steps and onto the sidewalk. He moves slowly toward his car, then stops and turns. "Oh, I found a house to look at. In New Holland. Can we go see it?"

"How about Monday?"

"Monday. That's good. Let's go Monday." He turns, waving over his shoulder, and climbs into his car.

I sit back down on the porch and watch him drive away. Again I consider the nature of friendship. Again I reflect on how busy I have become, how rare it is that I see the people I call friends. I think about where we've gone wrong, how we've ended up in this place where we make such little time for the people who mean the most to us, where we have almost no time for the people in our communities who need a place to sit and talk. A place to reflect on what it is they're missing.

Is friendship vanishing? Will we ever find the time for it again?

In his novel *The Great Divorce*, C. S. Lewis presents a picture in which all the inhabitants of hell are so disgusted with each other and angry and bitter and unforgiving that they keep moving farther and farther apart. Always farther apart, until it would take hundreds, even thousands, of years to journey through the space they have created between them.

Sometimes it feels that way, like we are all so busy, like we are all moving farther and farther apart.

18

Passing Each Other By

September 2017

I stop by to see Mohammad at the dry cleaner where he is still working. It's about ten minutes from the center of our small city, and I don't get out that way very often. My own life is hectic and hands me no spare time. Sometimes I wonder if I am equipped to be a good friend to someone who needs so much, especially when my own margins are so tight.

I pull into the parking lot and the sun is hot. It's a warm day in late August. The air is heavy, like an X-ray vest on the chest. I walk up to the dry cleaner, where a different kind of heat emanates through the propped-open door, smelling of chemicals and hard work. I watch for a moment through the glass. Mohammad is climbing a ladder and pulling on some kind of large conveyor belt that all the dry-cleaned clothes hang on. He spins it farther, looking for a particular garment. I look over into one of the side rooms and see Moradi hard at work.

Mohammad turns to ring up a customer. He sees me and grins. "Shawn!" He always says my name in a kind of exultant shout, as if he never expected to see me again but there I am, turning up when he least expects it. "One minute." He takes the customer's cash, gives change, and closes the drawer. He comes out from behind the counter.

"Hi, Mohammad," I say, smiling. "How are you?"

"I am hot." He chuckles, moving his company-branded T-shirt in and out, trying to fan some air against his body. "So hot. Moradi is in the back. How are you?"

There are no customers now, so he gestures toward a bench outside the store. We sit down.

"It is hot," he says again.

"Anything new with you?" I ask. "Is the bus coming for your children yet?"

"Not yet, not yet. But my friend, he is asking the school about it." He shrugs as if this is the least of his problems. "My oldest son, he is riding his bike to school. The others can walk. It is close."

"But what about this winter, when it gets cold?"

He shrugs again. "It will be fine. The bus will come. Or I will take him. Maybe Moradi. It will be fine."

I imagine that when your life concerns have included mortars hitting your house and surviving in a refugee camp, a school bus that does not show up can seem like a minor problem.

"I would like to find a house in the country," he says, his voice suddenly melancholy. "I want there to be grass and trees and space."

I try to encourage him, but our search has not turned up anything new. I'm not sure if he realizes how unlikely it is that he would be able to get into a property managed by a Realtor, and none of my friends or family have anything to rent. I keep asking, hoping, but I haven't made any progress.

"We'll find something," I say. "But for now, you have a nice place, right? You have a yard and space for the boys to run around. For the city, your house is a good house. Don't worry."

"I miss the country. I miss the quiet." He stares out over the parking lot. "Hey!" he shouts, as though suddenly remembering something. "Let's go to the beach."

"The beach?"

"Yes, the beach. Is it close?"

"I think you can get to a beach in a few hours."

"Let's go," he says again. "Your family. My family. All of us. This Sunday."

"This Sunday is Labor Day weekend," I explain. "It will be crazy. Too many people. How about next weekend?"

He nods. "I think that will work. I will check my work schedule."

Cars stream by. The sky is weighed down by the humidity and the heat. Moradi peeks her head out and says hello, wearing her black scarf over her head. She fans her face in an exaggerated fashion and we all chuckle, then she goes back to work.

"Have you ever been to the beach?" I ask Mohammad. "Have you ever seen the ocean?"

"I have been to the Arabian Sea," he says, "but no, I have never been to the ocean."

"Really?" I ask.

He shakes his head. "No."

"So, let's go to the beach."

I try to imagine his four boys running through the sand. They would love that. They would love the water and the sun.

But the weeks pass. His work schedule does not leave room for day trips, and my own work is pressing, overwhelming. I have deadlines and potential clients to meet with. We speak less as he enters the cycle of getting his boys to school and going to work and watching the children on the weekends while Moradi does housekeeping at the hotel.

We text. We talk quickly on the phone. I wonder if our friendship will last, or if it will fade as he finds his own way in this life and the busyness of my own sets in.

19

Income Requirements

It's a sunny day in September. Our goal of finding Mohammad's family a new home before the start of the school year hasn't happened. We're still looking. He still texts me photos of different houses nearly every day, and I call the Realtors.

"Hi," I say to one Realtor. "I'm calling about the house you're renting? My friend is looking for a place."

"Okay," the Realtor says, giving me the details. "Would your friend like to come and see it?"

"Sure," I say. "He's a Syrian refugee. He's been paying $1,000-per-month rent on time or early for the last year. He'd like to move out of the city."

Silence on the other end of the line. A clearing of the throat. A pause.

"Okay, well, he'll need to fill out an online application. And please be sure to take a look at the income requirement."

"How much is that?" I ask.

"We require a monthly income of at least three to four times the rent."

"And the rent here is $1,200?"

"That's correct."

"So, you're only renting to people who make around $36,000 to $50,000 a year?"

A pause, then, "Yes, that's correct."

I say thanks and hang up.

I never realized before now how difficult it is for someone to get into a rental house. When I was a kid, growing up in the country surrounded by fields and old friends and family, you could usually find a place to live that was rented out by someone you knew. Rental application—what was that? Income requirements—what? You moved in. You paid rent. You told them when you were going to leave.

This is a new situation. I'm starting to think Mohammad won't be able to find a place to live outside the city, not with his income, not with his $9.50-an-hour job. Still, we go look at places. As usual, he has hope.

———

I pull up outside of his house and he comes out, still in his dry cleaner work uniform. He grins, pulls out a soda, and climbs into the car.

"Mohammad!" I say. "How are you?" It's been a week or so since we've seen each other. He always looks so happy. He's one of the most positive people I've ever met.

"Good! Good. Shawn, how are your children?"

"Everyone's well. Are you ready to look at a house?"

We head out. The place we're looking at today is a small town house about thirty minutes north of the city. I'm not entirely sure why we're looking at it—Mohammad would need to find a new job if he moved all the way out there, and because it's a property under management, there's an income requirement I can't imagine he would meet—but I figure it's good for him to see some different places, get a feel for the market.

As we drive out of the city, heading out into the country, he takes in the fields and the farms. He watches the land go by like a child who has never seen such wide-open spaces. I keep glancing over at him as we drive without saying anything for a long time. He takes a call and chatters on in Arabic, then hangs up.

"This is what it is like in my village!" he says, excitedly motioning toward the fields and the hills. He sits back in his seat with something like relief. "I would like to live here. This is a good place."

We talk about where he came from. He tells me the story of when he found out about the program that resettled Syrian refugees to the United States.

"I didn't think it would happen," he says. "There were too many of us in Jordan. How would we be chosen? But then she called again, six months later, the same girl I spoke with before. She asked again if we wanted to leave Jordan, and again I told her yes, very much. She asked if we would like to go to the United States." He laughs, shakes his head. "I told her yes, very much, but I never thought it could happen. She hung up again, and I didn't hear from her for another month. The next time she called, she told me to come to meet her, just me, by myself."

"What did you think?" I ask. "Did you finally believe it could happen?"

"Still no. I didn't think so. But I went. After I arrived, she gathered my paperwork together. We didn't talk very much. She looked at everything I had written, and then I left. The next time she called, she asked me to bring in my family. So Moradi and the boys and I all went into the office. We had a short meeting, and that was it. We left. I still didn't know. One month later, she called and said people from the United States wanted to meet with us."

I try to imagine what it would be like if I was the one going through that. I try to imagine moving to the Middle East, to Syria or Jordan or Iraq, and going into a meeting that would determine if I could move away from a war zone and into a place of peace. I try to imagine how intimidated I would feel, how nervous, how desperate.

"Were you nervous? Did they ask a lot of questions?"

He shakes his head in disbelief. "So many questions, Shawn! So many questions. They asked security questions. They asked me anything. Everything! They started from when I was a boy, where I lived, who my friends were. Where did I work? How many brothers and sisters did I have? Why did I want to go to the United States? Did I have any problems in Jordan? On and on."

"Did you have any problems in Jordan?" I ask, laughing.

"No! None at all. Then he asked the names of all my brothers and sisters, which is hard to remember, because there are fourteen of us."

"Fourteen!"

"Yes." He laughs, slapping his leg at the hilarity of it all. "Too many names—you know, sometimes I cannot even list my brothers and sisters! They even asked about my cousins. They wanted to know the names of my cousins. They asked so many questions. And we had to go back to the office again and again. Each time they asked us new questions, and sometimes they asked the same ones over and over. You would not believe how many questions they asked us. And they asked Moradi the same questions, to make sure we gave the same answers."

"Wow."

We drive farther north. This is Amish country, and we pass them in their fields, wagons pulled by horses, young children helping to bring in the harvest of hay or alfalfa or corn bales. There are fields of soybeans. The tobacco is turning golden in these end-of-summer days. Mohammad takes it all in, drinks it all up.

"I like this," he says quietly to himself as we head north. "This is good. Yes."

"How long did the process take?" I ask him, but he doesn't understand the question. "When did this woman call you to see if you wanted to go to the United States?"

"Oh, yes. In January she called, and it took a year and a half. In July 2016 we arrived. At first they asked us if we wanted to go to Canada or Australia. I do not know why they chose America in the end. But I am happy."

"Did Moradi want to come to the United States? Was she worried about coming here?"

"Did Moradi want to come?" he echoes, nodding. "She wanted to come more than me! I wasn't sure if we should move so far from home, away from the Middle East, but she wanted to come for the boys. For our boys. She asked me what we would do if we stayed in Jordan. Where would I work? Where would the boys go to school? There was no life there. She said all of this. And the war is always in Syria—we cannot go back there."

He pauses, nodding, reminiscing.

"Yes, I remember. She said, 'Everything is broken now. But if we go to the United States, the future is good for the boys. Here in Jordan or in Syria, there is nothing for them. Nothing. In the United States, they could be doctors. They could do something with their lives. Here they can do nothing. In the US, maybe something.' Then I said, 'Okay. Let's go.'"

We pull into a small town house community. There is a neighboring park, and railroad tracks line the back of the property. I park and we wait for the Realtor.

"In Jordan, people knew we were Syrian, and some of them treated us poorly. The first place we lived, the first city, we were not welcome. The boys were treated poorly," he says, as if these are things he would rather not talk about, things he would rather forget. "But then, at the last place we lived in Jordan, I was asking myself why we didn't move there sooner! They were very nice. Very kind. And these were two different cities in the same country. I guess some people are different."

A car pulls into the lot. A man gets out, and I assume he's the Realtor.

"When we knew we were coming to the States," Mohammad continues, "our neighbors there came together with us and were crying because we were leaving. That was the difference between Ajloun and Irbid. They cried for us there when we left."

"Were you nervous about coming to the States?" I ask.

"Afraid? I was not afraid. I was coming to a new life." He shrugs as if entering a new life is something we all do, as if it's no big deal. "I was not afraid. But you know something? I was coming to the United States. I have friends who went to Germany or France or Canada, and years have passed and they're still not working!

There are no jobs, or the country requires them to take years of language classes. I can learn while I work. This is what I like about the United States. I can work. We have a life. This is good."

We get out of the car and walk over to the house. The door is open, and I peek inside. "Hello?"

The Realtor comes around the corner. He introduces himself. Mohammad and I take off our shoes and walk around the house.

"This is nice," Mohammad says quietly as we wander from room to room.

"It's only three bedrooms," I say. "You and Moradi would be in one. Would you put two boys in each of the other bedrooms?"

"No, no." He explains that his oldest son, who is fourteen now, could have the small bedroom to himself. The two middle boys would share a room, and their youngest would sleep in their room.

"He still sleeps with you?" I ask, laughing.

He smiles. I can tell he has a soft spot for their youngest boy.

We go back downstairs, and the Realtor explains the application process. The rent is $1,000 a month, the same amount he has paid on time every month since they arrived in the United States.

"What's the income requirement?" I ask.

"We like to see an income of at least three times the rent."

I thank him and we go back out to the car.

"It's a nice house," Mohammad says quietly. "But it's very far from work. Too far. I don't know."

"We can keep looking," I say.

The drive home is quiet. We reenter the city, and the hustle, the movement, the cars, the people—all of it feels comforting somehow. It's good to get lost here, among the buildings, among all these stories.

20

Smiling through It All

October 2017

A few days pass. Another week. A month. It's Sunday night, and I'm tired.

Our oldest two require a nearly full-time taxi service, and our youngest are still getting up in the night. We wander from day to day like the barely undead, catching ten-minute naps in the car or on the couch, crossing paths on our way into sleep each night. This is not a complaint. This is life. It's good. It's a blessing. It's exhausting.

Mohammad and I have been trying to get together all weekend, and I know that if I don't go see him now, another week will come and go in a blur. So at 8:00 p.m., once my kids are asleep and Maile is reading a book in bed, I get in the car and cruise south on Prince Street, past King, and right on Hazel, back into Mohammad's neighborhood. It's a dark night. The streets are mostly empty and the sky is clouded over.

I park outside and walk to the front door, which is in between the tall, leaning flowers Mohammad and his wife planted along the sidewalk earlier that summer. I think again about how their neighborhood is a nice one. These duplexes have small yards, two levels, a parking space in the back. I know he wants to move to the country, but it could be worse. This is a nice part of the city.

I knock on the door and hear the scurry of little feet. His sons answer the door, all four of them at once, jostling for position.

"Shawn!" they cry out in their varying degrees of Arabic accents. The older boys, middle-school age, are finding American voices. I wonder how their parents feel about that—is it a relief to know your children will fit in, or is there a sadness in realizing that their voices will never be like yours? When we had attended the refugee welcome at the nightclub, one of the boys tried to write something in Arabic. He couldn't remember how to write the letters, and Mohammad had stepped in and patiently shown him. His own son did not know how to write in the language he himself had grown up speaking. I try to imagine being thrust into a situation where my own children can't write English words. It's almost impossible to envision.

The older two speak English fluently and the younger two are learning English fast. They have all started their second year in school in the US. I hope this year will be easier on everyone. When I think back to the previous year—arriving in a new country, a new school, barely speaking the language—I realize there is no way it could be more difficult. This year will be better, as will every year from here on out. I'm relieved they have made it through those difficult beginnings.

"Hey, guys!" I laugh, give high fives, and pat the youngest on the head. He is five or maybe six years old, a spitfire, a ball of energy. His dark eyes hold mischief of the highest order and his limbs are always moving. He's always on the verge of breaking something—the coffee table, the television, one of his own bones. It's also quite clear he is the apple of his father's eye.

"Where's your dad?" I ask.

"He's in the kitchen," one of them says, so I follow the four of them around the corner. Mohammad is grinding coffee with a small grinder, pouring each batch of coffee into a tall, plastic container. It smells delicious. I wonder if he's preparing for the week ahead, getting his coffee ready for his early mornings.

Recently I asked him about his morning schedule. What time does he wake up? What time do the boys wake up? He told me he gets up at 5:30—he cannot sleep any later. He says his prayers, he makes coffee, he goes out on the back patio and sits in silence. Then, at 7:00, he wakes up the rest of the family.

This seems like a good routine. Prayers every morning. Sitting outside. I would benefit from saying more prayers. I would benefit from waking up early.

"Hello, Shawn," Mohammad says, shaking my hand and putting his other hand on my shoulder. "It is good to see you. Thank you for coming. Come. Sit."

We move back into the living room, and I sit on one of their couches. The boys are busy, always moving, going quickly from video games to computer games to sitting on the sofa and smiling, talking, laughing. Mohammad tells me of his latest escapades in the attempt to get the work he needs done on his teeth. One dentist is telling him he should have all his teeth pulled and get dentures. Another, for a much more affordable amount, has recommended a top and bottom bridge to fill the gaps. Mohammad is uncertain. Insurance might cover total replacement, but the bridge is cheaper.

We are friends now. We know what to talk about. It hasn't always been this way. Once we were strangers. When we first met, we sat in silence a fair bit, our English not always compatible. He was so new to the country. I find it remarkable now when I think back on just how new he was. What do you talk about with someone who is just learning what a quarter is? What car insurance is? Where to go for stamps? In the beginning, conversations can be halting, quick, jumping from one thing to the next. But now we know each other's lives. He asks about my children. I ask about Moradi's job.

He looks at his watch. "I must go!" he says suddenly. He stands, grabs a light jacket, and slips into his shoes. "Don't leave! Shawn! Don't leave. Wait until I get back. I must pick up Moradi from work."

"Go, go," I say. He leaves me and the boys at the house. They bring me a cup of their strong Turkish coffee, and in its dark depths I see a sleepless night ahead. Oh well. I sip it—it's hot as lava. The boys ask if I want sugar.

"Yes, please," I reply, and they grin, bringing me a whole cupful. "Thank you," I say, then ask them, "How is school going?"

Number one and number three are loving school. There are twenty-five kids in each of their classes. They like their teachers. Number three is taking English classes after school.

Number one grins and gloats. "I know my English. I don't have to stay after school for that."

We laugh.

I turn to one of their other sons. "And you? How is school going for you?"

He shrugs. "The boys pushed me out of my classroom today," he says, a dazed look on his face, a shallow smile. It's almost as if he's confessing something he doesn't want to. The other boys return to doing whatever it was they were doing, as if they're uncomfortable with what has happened and don't want to hear a story in which their family is not completely accepted in this new country.

"Really?" I ask. I feel empty. I want to go into his class and bang those boys' heads together. If they only knew what this young man has been through. I imagine the long walk he took through the wilderness, weighed down by backpacks full of food and water. I see again the hole left by the bomb that hit their house. I picture the endless sea of white tents in the refugee camp where they stayed. I think of the long years in Jordan, marked only by an ever-present boredom and nothing to alleviate it.

"I told the police officer in my school," he says, again shrugging and half-smiling. He is the smiler of the group. He reminds me of my daughter Abra, who will smile even when telling you of her greatest disappointment.

"What did he say? Did he do anything?" I want him to come sit beside me so I can put my arm around his shoulders and tell him to keep his head up, but I don't know if that's proper in their culture.

"He said he would talk to them." He tries to sound happy, tries to sound convinced.

I sigh. "Don't let them push you around." I pause. "You're a good kid."

He nods, smiles, nods again. I wonder if he understands what I'm saying, if he understands the word *kid*.

———

Mohammad returns with Moradi, who carries a vase of flowers in one hand and a tissue in the other. Her nose is red and she's coughing.

"Hi, Moradi," I say. "Maile says hello."

She gives a sad, tired smile. "Oh, thank you." She is still working on her English. During the week, she works with Mohammad at the dry cleaner. On Saturday and Sunday, she works at the hotel, cleaning rooms. She is a small woman and comes across as meek, but there is also something fierce about her, an underlying strength. I would not want to cross her.

Mohammad sits down beside me, and as we talk about how he wants to move into the country, his youngest son crowds in on his lap. He wants something—I cannot tell what—and they chatter at each other in Arabic. Mohammad is so tender with his boys, and even when his youngest sits close and talks so that his mouth bumps his father's cheek, Mohammad still smiles. He talks firmly, but there is a softness there too. Mohammad alternates between a growling voice and a purring one. He is a lion swatting away the cub, then welcoming it back, then swatting again.

That's when I recognize one word the little boy is using, hidden among the chatter of his Arabic. It's a word that leaps out to me, a word I have heard before but never in the wild. Never being used in its native language.

Abba.

"Abba," he begins pleading in a soft voice before chattering on in Arabic.

Abba. I have never heard this word used between an Arabic father and son before. Of course, in my Christian upbringing, much was said about the word, how Jesus encouraged his disciples to call God *Abba.* But I have never heard it like this. I have never heard a young boy say it, his face so close to his father's that they must be breathing the same air. His eyes pleading. His father smiling and kissing his cheeks and still saying no, but in such a loving way.

Abba.

An hour passes. Then two.

"Mohammad," I say, "I really have to go." It's now 10:00 p.m. A long week awaits.

Of course, Mohammad starts into his typical protestations. "Shawn!" he exclaims as if I have just insulted him in the greatest possible way. "No! Don't go. You cannot go."

"I have little children at home," I say. "I don't like leaving my wife at home alone with them. It's a lot of work." I wonder if everyone has stayed in bed. I wonder if I'll find a houseful of wandering children or if it will be quiet, still.

He resists for a few more moments, then eventually gives in, shrugging and acting as if he has only just now found it in his heart to forgive me for leaving his home after spending only two hours with him. We shake hands.

"Thank you, Shawn," he says, and his voice is so true and so transparent. I realize again and again how much it means to him—this simple presence, this basic friendship.

But it also has become so much to me. I realize that in most of my friendships, so little is required of either party. In America, we've valued independence for so long that we haven't recognized the gradual slipping into loneliness. Now we fend for ourselves, depending on no one, asking nothing, and, because of that, receiving so little.

With Mohammad, I receive so much.

I walk out into the dark, between the flowers. There is no moon, no stars. There are only the streetlights, and lonely people walking through the shadows, and cars leaving the city for who knows where.

Part Three

The Neighbor

"Now which of these three would you say was a neighbor to the man who was attacked by bandits?" Jesus asked.

The man replied, "The one who showed him mercy."

Then Jesus said, "Yes, now go and do the same."

Luke 10:36–37

21

Let's Be Neighbors

October 2017

Mohammad and I are on our way to Philadelphia on a quest to find him new teeth. His broken bottom bridge has not been fixed, and he's lived without it for a long time. So far, his insurance has not come through. He tells me he has not eaten meat in eight months. He laughs when he says it, as if missing teeth are the least of his worries.

Finding a dentist who takes Mohammad's insurance, one who can do the extensive work required for an amount Mohammad can afford, has been a significant challenge. We drive south out of the city even though Philadelphia lies more or less directly east, because it is not much farther if we go south, and the fields open up in that direction. East, everything is cement and pavement and strip malls, traffic and tension and less air to breathe. South, we will roll through farmers' fields and towns named Willow Street and Quarryville and Oxford. Even the highway down there, once we are finally on it, splits through the hills, and we can sneak up on Philadelphia when it's not looking.

"Ah," Mohammad says with a sigh and a grin as we leave the city behind us. "This is nice, Shawn. Shawn! This is nice. This is where I want to live."

He tells me about growing up as the child of a Muslim farmer in a small Syrian village in the seventies.

"We did everything by hand," he says. "We did not have machinery like they have today. It was hard work, and we used a . . ." He makes a motion with his hand that somehow indicates to me a knife.

"A scythe?" I ask.

"Yes, yes. We used a scythe to harvest. Long days. It was like the Amish here. My parents grew wheat and chickpeas. The chickpea plant is a small plant. Everyone in the village did that—everyone was a farmer. The government would buy our crops, come and take them away. You cannot sell to a company or a person. You have to sell to the government."

"Did you have time to play when you were a boy, or was it always work?"

"At 4:00 on most afternoons, all of the boys from our area would meet up and play soccer. All together, my friends and my neighbors and my cousins, we would meet. Just the boys. Sometimes we would play with the girls, but not just any girls—only cousins or sisters. Not just any girls."

He motions toward his foot and makes a mini kicking motion, then he slaps his leg and laughs. "That was fun. Those were good days."

"And what about your parents? What were they like?" I ask.

"My parents?"

"Yes, your mother and father. What were they like? How did they treat you?"

"My father, he was happy. He was also very, very serious. Very strict. A good father. A strict father. He was like every other father I knew. He expected us to work hard, to do things right, and if you didn't, he shouted. Sometimes . . ." He swings his hand.

"You'd get a smack?"

He shrugs. "This is how all fathers were in Syria then. If he asked you to do something and you didn't do it, he shouted. He was sometimes angry. Look, every father in my country is the same. My father is not alone—all the people are like that. 'Do this! Do that!'"

"And your mother?"

"My mother was also like all the mothers. All the time, everywhere, the mothers, my mom, any mom, is very nice with children. Very different from the fathers. So kind and sweet and gentle. She did not say much. This was my mother."

There are times, as we drive through the countryside, when neither of us speaks. I do not turn on the radio. All I can hear is the whir of the tires on the pavement. The sun is hot through the windows, though the day is all October. The leaves are changing. The fields are mostly empty.

Mohammad drinks up the countryside, thirsty for the space. I know he misses his mother. He speaks of her often.

"Shawn, when you buy a house down here, find one for me too. We will live here and here." He points to two houses close together. "We can have coffee all the time."

He laughs. I laugh. It's true—my wife and I are thinking of selling our house and moving south of the city. We have six children, and our oldest two have somehow morphed into the physical form of adults. We could use more outside space, a place to cast them all out into when a day requires it.

"That sounds great," I say.

And we keep driving south.

———

"When you were a kid, was Syria at war?" I ask.

"No, no, no. I was born in 1971. In 1973, there was a war between Syria and Israel, but I do not remember it, and I never saw it. No one in my village ever saw that war. This war is the first I have ever seen, the first war my village has ever seen. And now it is a war not against my enemy but against my friend. Fellow Syrians. Why is this happening? I don't know."

This is a new thought to me, that someone could grow up in the Middle East and have a peaceful life. When I watch the news, it seems that every country in that region has been involved in war since what seems like the beginning of time. There's something more poignant to me about Mohammad's story, knowing that he went through childhood, through his teenage years, and well into his adulthood in a peaceful place. That's me. That's my story and the story of my family.

What would I do if a civil war broke out in my country? Would I stay and fight? If not, where would I go?

"How did this all begin in your village?"

"Some people went outside. They thought the government had been overthrown, and they went outside and celebrated. Only some people. But this didn't last long. And in the beginning, it was slow, slow, slow. It didn't all happen at once, but it just kept getting worse and worse.

"The first person from my village who was killed was an eighteen-year-old. He went to Dara'a. The government had surrounded it with a blockade, and no one could go inside or outside. Some people from my village went to a village close to Dara'a, because they knew people there who needed bread, needed food, needed water. But I didn't go. Many others went. They wanted to break through and get to Dara'a. This village was called Sidah.

"When the people arrived, there was a large army. A government army. They let everyone in, and the streets were full of people. Thousands. Tens of thousands. Twenty thousand, maybe? I don't know how many. When this young man, the one from our village, went into Sidah, when he got into the middle, this was when the army opened fire into the crowd. I think the government killed 129 people. Something like that. Many, many people. Three or four thousand were injured. I don't know. This eighteen-year-old was killed."

The word *killed* floats in the air around us. The other words find a way out of the car and we leave them behind in the fields, but the word *killed* is not so easily disposed of. It is a heavy word. It takes the air. It quiets us.

"I stayed home," he says. "I was sleeping. Everyone in the village was out in the streets again after the boy was killed."

"Why didn't you go?" I ask. "Why did you stay home if other people from your village went to see what was going on?"

"I didn't want to get involved. Some people, Shawn, some people . . . I have seen this before. I have seen the Arabic governments do these things. I live in Syria—I don't live in Germany or Switzerland! I know this man, Assad."

For a moment his voice trails off, as if he's trying to decide how to say this in a way that will convince me.

"I know this man, Assad, and his father, and all of the other leaders like him. I know he will kill you. They don't care. You don't know. This is hard for you to understand, maybe. The government in Syria is not good, and the army is not good. I didn't live in the United States or England. I lived in Syria. You cannot trust the government there."

"Why did the soldiers open fire?"

He shrugs. "They didn't want the people to go from Sidah to Dara'a. They wanted to stop it there and end it, and everything would go back to normal. This, maybe, is what they thought."

"That's it?"

"That's it."

The miles fly behind us, and we start heading east and a little north, approaching Philadelphia. He is quiet for a long time.

"After that, when these things happened in Sidah, rebels started coming to our town. Any village or city where the rebels were, they would tell the government people to leave and then they would fire bombs in. Shooting bombs at everyone without even aiming.

"We would hear that these bombings were going to take place. The people we knew who worked in the local government warned us, warned everyone. So I would take my family to another village. For a long time we went to this other village almost every day. By now I had sold my car and all I had was my motorcycle. Just my motorcycle. I would get onto it with Moradi and all four boys! All six of us on one motorcycle, and our youngest was so little." He shakes his head and smiles in disbelief. "All six of us."

"All of you on the motorcycle?"

"All of us!"

"Where would you go?"

"We went to a neighboring village that was both Christian and Muslim. We had friends there, and we stayed with them. There were also other friends with us, friends who lived in our village. Sometimes the men would sit on their porch and watch the bombs hit our village off in the distance. 'Oh,' I would say, 'was that your house?' And we would watch. 'I think that was your house,' my friend would say. We watched the bombs fall on our village. We watched our houses getting hit, but we were very far away, so we couldn't know for sure."

He laughs at this crazy game of watching their houses being hit by bombs, the juxtaposition of sitting on a friend's patio quietly drinking coffee while your own government shoots mortars into your village.

"Sometimes we would go home right away, and sometimes we would spend the night. I had a friend who would call and tell me when the bombing was over, when it was safe. When we returned one evening, we found our house had been hit. A mortar had gone through the cement-block wall into our dining room, where we ate. I spackled over the hole with cement. After that, every time my children left the house, I stared at that spackled wall and wondered if they would come back home safe. I did. I was scared. Very, very scared."

He is serious now. "I used to shake when I spoke about these things," he says, holding out one of his hands to show me. "I used to be very nervous talking about the bombing of my village, but now it does not bother me anymore. See? I am not shaking."

He stares at his hands, appearing amazed at what time can do, amazed at how years can take away the outward signs of fear and anxiety. He sighs and rubs his eyes. There is a deep, deep sadness there, something like tears but not visible. Something heavy that cannot be seen.

"You know, Shawn," he says with a wistful look on his face, staring straight ahead as we drive, "I still cannot believe this happened to us. I am sitting here telling you about my village. My village! My village was bombed! Sometimes people do not believe me when I tell them this. Even people from Syria do not believe me. I still cannot believe it myself. I am telling you about it, but I cannot believe it is true."

———

The city of Philadelphia rises up around us subtly, first as suburbs, then as heavy traffic, then as bridges spanning great spaces filled with smoke-belching factories. Finally, as the distant metropolis grows near, high-rises pierce the blue sky. I wonder if Mohammad could make this drive on his own. The signs are not incredibly clear all the time—merging at the last minute is a must in some cases.

I realize I'm thinking about him much the same way a parent thinks of a teenager about to get their driver's license.

Would he have seen that sign?

Would he have understood that U-turn?

Would he remember where to park, where not to park?

We meander into the outskirts of Philadelphia, where the row home–lined streets are grids as far as the eye can see. We find the small dentist's office in a row of other small businesses and park in a thirty-minute spot. Inside, the receptionist peppers him with questions about his ID and insurance and forms that must be filled out. The dentist comes out, and he is young. Much younger than I expected.

He speaks to Mohammad in Arabic, and the two smile at each other the way you might smile upon returning home after a long absence. They chatter on and on. Mohammad is clearly excited to travel two hours, all the way to a faraway city, to find someone who speaks his own language, someone who knows his home country.

The dentist turns to me and speaks perfect English without an accent. "You brought Mohammad?"

I nod.

"How long did it take you?"

"Maybe an hour and a half," I say. "Maybe a little longer. Traffic wasn't too bad."

"I thought it might be two or three hours," he says. "I didn't know if it would be worth it for him to make such a long journey. Thank you for helping him."

I shrug. "He's a friend. It's no problem."

The dentist is Syrian. He moved to the United States in 2008, attended school in Nashville, and decided on a whim not to return in 2011, even when most other Syrians were heartened by the improvements taking place, the peace. Many of his friends returned to Syria in those days, when peace felt close. Now those same friends are stuck there, trying to get out, or biding their time in remote villages, hoping the current quiet transforms into a lasting peace.

"Do you think you can help Mohammad?" I ask him.

"We're going to get him signed up," he says, smiling. He has a kind smile. "I think we'll be able to help him."

I wonder if it feels to him like he's helping his father or an uncle. I wonder about the cultural ties that bind people who find themselves in foreign lands. I wonder what I would do if I came across another American in some faraway country, both of us having fled our home during a civil war. I'm sure I would go out of my way to help.

Mohammad goes into one of the examination rooms and I walk across the street to a very large, very empty diner. City traffic creeps past on the side roads, ekes its way out of side alleys. I sit at the mostly empty bar and read a book on my phone. I feel the vacancy only cities can bestow, the loneliness that happens when you're surrounded by a city full of strangers.

———

Mohammad calls me forty-five minutes later to tell me his appointment is finished and to meet him at the corner. He has found someone who sells the flatbread he and his family eat at every meal, so he'd like to stock up. When I pull up to the corner store, he comes out carrying a few dozen clear plastic bags full of the bread. He is grinning from ear to ear as he loads it into the back seat.

"It's a little expensive," he says, shrugging. "But this is good. This is good."

We drive away, slowly finding our way out of the city. He gives me an update on what the dentist is recommending, how they will be able to help, and the various people he will need to call to get the correct insurance. It seems so complicated.

The drive home is mostly silent. He calls his boys to see if Moradi has come home from work yet. He takes a call from his brother-in-law and they talk loudly back and forth in Arabic. The miles pass, and soon we are back in the countryside between Philadelphia and Lancaster, approaching our home from the south.

"You know," he says, "in Syria, we are always having coffee together. Almost every day I went to a friend's house and we sat for two hours, for three hours, drinking coffee together, talking about things. Why do you not do that here? Everyone stays here, here, here." He frowns and jabs at the air. "No one knows their neighbors. No one has coffee."

"You're right," I say. "You're right."

"I tell this to Moradi," he says, giving a reluctant smile. "I tell her I will start having coffee with people. Soon everyone will come to my house and we will all know each other and talk together. She says, 'Mohammad, Americans do not want this! They do not want!' But I tell her I will show her. I will start. We will meet here, there. Maybe at a coffeehouse. It is good this way, for us to drink coffee together." He laughs.

I laugh too, but the truth of what he says reaches me. We as Americans are very good at being independent. I struggle to think of the last time I needed someone, truly needed someone. We are so busy. Too busy. There is very little time for that kind of community, where we meet together regularly, unrushed, to simply drink coffee.

"When you find a house out here . . ." Mohammad says. He laughs again, showing that boyish grin of his. "Find me a house too. We will live beside each other, and we will drink coffee together. We can invite all the neighbors!"

22

Bring Me Your Tired

July 13, 2016

Mohammad's family of six arrived in the United States on July 13, 2016. He remembers this date and recalls it easily, like a birthday. He always knows his proximity from it—if I ask him how long he has been in the States, he can answer immediately, down to the number of days. It is a date in his life that serves as a marker—everything has happened to him either before or after that date.

Late on that July night, the six of them swam in a sea of people, surrounded by languages and ethnicities and a summer New York heat that moved through the airport in waves. Mohammad held their youngest boy close, and it was like crossing through the Jordanian wilderness again, keeping everyone together, moving everyone in the right direction. Moradi looked around anxiously, pulling her covering close. Their other three boys looked around wide-eyed, simultaneously excited and terrified by the noise, the hustle and bustle, the people going here and there and everywhere. They had never seen anything like it before in their lives.

The family walked along on that late night in New York City's JFK Airport, exhausted, overstimulated, and looking for the woman they were supposed to meet. They had arrived on a plane full of Syrian refugees, they had all wandered together in a loose conglomerate through customs, and now they would all go their separate ways. Some would go on to the West Coast, becoming Californians. Some would go north, their children growing up with snow and white Christmases. Some would go south, where the weather reminded them of home. And some, like Mohammad and his family, would stay in the Mid-Atlantic states. A seemingly random choice by someone, somewhere, determined where these families would end up, the friends they would meet, the weather they would become used to, and the paths their children would take.

Each refugee had a lanyard. At the top it read, in bold, "International Organization for Migration." Below that it had a series of blanks filled in:

To Whom It May Concern:
   My name is:
   I am a refugee from:
   I may not speak English and need help to find my next flight.
   If there is any problem or emergency please call IOM New York and refer to this information:
   Or you may contact my sponsor in Lancaster, PA:

Mohammad looked at his lanyard and spun it around for the hundredth time so that the words faced out. His gaze swept the crowd again, a tired stare. He knew very little English, really only a few words. How would he find his way in this sea of people? He did not know where to go, so they stood and waited.

They did not wait long. A woman emerged from the crowd, rounding up all the Syrian refugees who had arrived that night. She was energetic and welcoming. She smiled a lot and spoke Arabic.

"Come with me," she said in a happy voice. "We're going to put you in a hotel for the night. Tomorrow you all will head on to your final destinations."

Mohammad approached her hesitantly. "I am supposed to go to Lancaster?" he asked.

"Tomorrow," she replied. "Tomorrow we will make sure you get to your city."

The crowd of refugees fell in behind her, staying close to their family members, and they all walked out toward the sidewalk. Mohammad and the boys pulled their luggage along behind them. But as they started walking, another pair came up to them, a woman and a man.

"Mohammad?" she asked, looking at his name tag.

"Yes?" he said, using one of the only words he knew.

"Mohammad! Welcome to the United States!" she said in a kind voice, shaking his hand, then giving Moradi a hug and greeting the boys. "I am from CWS in Lancaster. We are here to take you home."

He was confused. He didn't know what she was saying. Then suddenly the man who was with her began speaking Arabic, just as the other woman had. They had found the people from CWS! Tears filled his eyes, and he reached out and shook the man's hand with both of his. A feeling of comfort washed over him, and the edges of his anxiety dulled.

"I think . . ." Mohammad began, trying to come up with the English words, but the translator jumped in again. He told Mohammad there had been a mix-up. They had come to take him and his family to Lancaster that night. They would leave immediately.

"Okay," Mohammad said. "Okay."

They went out to a van and climbed inside. The boys were tired. The flight from Jordan to Cairo, Egypt, had taken a few hours. The flight from Cairo to New York had been thirteen hours. The drive from New York City to Lancaster would take three hours. They didn't say much during that last leg of the journey. The boys leaned their heads against the side of the vehicle and fell asleep. Moradi pulled her veil close around her face and drifted off, her head swaying gently with the movement of the van.

Mohammad could not sleep. He could not believe it. They had finally arrived in the United States, and they were only a few hours from their new home. He had expected to wake up still in his bed in Jordan, still wondering how in the world he would make a future for his boys. But they were in the US. They were in that future. He smiled to himself and looked back at the boys, all of them asleep, their mouths hanging open, their eyes lightly closed.

This is good, he thought. *We did the right thing.*

———

They drove the long, dark journey through New Jersey and eastern Pennsylvania. So many trees. So many stars. So many miles. They arrived at their home in Lancaster at around 1:00, and when they got out of the car, Mohammad stood there for a moment in the darkness. His house was on the edge of the city, and he stared toward the lights to the northeast. A few buildings rose up into the sky.

He was amazed at the silence.

Christina, the CWS employee, showed them around the house and answered their questions, staying with them until nearly 2:00. The house already had furniture. Everything had been provided by local families: plates, chairs, beds. There was even food in the pantry and in the refrigerator, chosen by a local Syrian family who had arrived months before Mohammad's family. It was nice to know there were others like them close by. He wondered when his family could meet them.

Christina and the translator left. Mohammad and his family found beds or space on the floor and collapsed, exhausted. But Mohammad slept lightly, aware of every noise, listening for who knows what. Anything. Everything. It was a new country, a new neighborhood, and he couldn't help but be on high alert. Was it a safe neighborhood? Would people here accept them, as they had been accepted in the last Jordanian village, or would they be outcasts, confined to this small house? He had high hopes, but still, he listened. Eventually even he fell asleep.

The noises Mohammad heard in the morning, around 7:00, immediately woke him. He listened intently. There was a tapping, then it stopped. He waited and it started again. It got louder, and off in the distance he heard voices. Someone was inside his house.

He crept from the bed and walked carefully to the stairway. He walked gingerly down the stairs, trying not to make a noise. This was unexpected. He had hoped America would be a safe place for his family. How was he supposed to call the police? What was the number? Who did he ask for? And if he reached the police, how would he tell them where to go? He tried to remember where the lady from CWS had put the paper with all of his information.

Another loud bang, followed by the sound of . . . a drill? What was going on?

He peeked around the corner at the bottom of the steps, and there was a man and a boy in his house! He gathered his courage.

"Hello?" he asked, his voice trembling. "Hello?"

The man looked up, surprised. "You're here already?"

Mohammad nodded without understanding what the man was saying. Then he shrugged.

"I'm the owner of the house! No one told me you would be here today."

Mohammad was uncertain. Was he not supposed to be in the house? He and the man stumbled over their words as they tried to communicate, the man waving his arms, repeating himself louder.

"I need to fix the water in the bathroom," the man said. "Water. In the bathroom."

"Ah," Mohammad said, relaxing. "Sorry?"

"No! Don't apologize. I didn't know you would be here already. I thought you were coming tonight."

Mohammad walked the rest of the way into the room and the men shook hands. Mohammad made coffee in his new kitchen, looking here and there for things, opening and closing cupboards. So this was what his new life would be like. This was where things were located.

When the man finished working, he sat on the back porch with Mohammad and they drank coffee together. After a few halting attempts at conversation, the two gave up, but still they sat there, drinking coffee, enjoying the morning.

Mohammad looked out at his new neighborhood, at the street where cars occasionally passed, at the distant buildings. He looked up at the blue sky and the green trees. Everything was so different from the Middle East. So different. Again he thought that perhaps he was still in a dream. He knew he had woken up, but perhaps he had woken up to another dream? Maybe none of it was true. Maybe he was still in Jordan, living in a small apartment, not allowed to work, his boys unable to go to school. Maybe he was dreaming of freedom because he was, in fact, still trapped.

But no. The dream did not fade. He was in America. It was true.

For two or three days, he still thought he might be in a dream.

Everything in my life is different now, he often thought. *Everything.*

———

On that first day in Lancaster, Moradi and the boys slept in, exhausted from the long journey. What a day that had been! One moment they were in Jordan, and less than twenty-four hours later, they were situated in Lancaster, beginning their new life.

Eventually the family stirred, came downstairs, ate breakfast. They gave long yawns that ended in smiles and walked around the house in a jetlagged haze. The boys explored. They wanted to go outside, but Mohammad was nervous, not knowing the area, so they all went for a walk together to see this new place, this new home.

He decided to take the boys to a nearby park Christina had told them about, a mile away. It was a beautiful summer day—the leaves were bright green, the air was growing warmer, and the sky was blue. He and Moradi walked quietly together while the boys ran ahead. Their footsteps made soft, rhythmic sounds on the cement sidewalk, and for the first time, he was not afraid for them. They darted off toward the park once it came into view, and he did not call them back.

He realized they were safe. Finally safe. His family could grow here. In Jordan, they had stayed inside as much as possible wherever they were living, and their houses and apartments had become a prison to them. In Lancaster, he finally felt, for the first time in many years, that his family would be okay. They had a future now, a path laid out in front of them.

A weight lifted from him in that moment. There were still many hurdles ahead—many fears and unknown challenges—but he felt the beginning of their new life. And it was good.

Many months later, when we are no longer strangers, Mohammad tells me about that day.

"I will never forget it," he says, smiling almost in disbelief. "Our first day in Lancaster. The boys were running and jumping and having fun. They ran off ahead of us and I let them run." He smiles, a look of wonder on his face at the thought of his boys running free again.

He pauses.

"I will never forget that day."

When refugees arrive in the United States, their airfare is paid for by an interest-free loan program run by the International Organization for Migration (IOM). Before they leave for the US, refugees have to sign a promissory note stating that they will pay back the costs of their travel within a certain period. These loans and their repayment make it possible for more refugees to be resettled.

As soon as Mohammad arrived in the United States, he was determined to pay the loans back and become financially self-sufficient as soon as possible. But he couldn't work until he had an ID card and a Social Security number, so in order to stay busy while he waited for these documents, he walked the city streets. Christina and the translator from CWS showed him around. They taught him how to catch a bus and where the buses went, where to shop, where to buy things for his home.

Every day for the first two months, Mohammad walked the city. He found the schools the boys would attend. He kept his eye out for places to work. CWS helped him buy a car and find a doctor. As he wandered up Queen Street and down Prince Street, as he visited the market and took the bus to Walmart, as he met new people and crossed paths with other refugees who had been resettled in Lancaster, he felt something he hadn't felt for a long time.

Safe.

At the end of August, all four of Mohammad's boys started school. One of them took the bus. Two of them could walk, since the school was just around the corner. But he worried about his youngest boy. What if he needed to go to the bathroom and no one knew what he was saying? What if he was hungry and no one understood? What if he was thirsty? What if they did not treat him well?

Mohammad received permission from the school to sit in the back of his son's classroom all day, every day. The two of them headed out early in the morning, quietly walking the city streets with all of the other children on their way to school. The air smelled different then because it was fall, and the leaves were turning and the heat was sliding away.

In the classroom, Mohammad took up his seat at the back, and he listened to the teacher and watched over his youngest boy, making sure he behaved, making sure he was understood. He learned a bit of English there, listening. After a few weeks, Mohammad realized his son would be okay.

At about that time, Moradi was told about a job at a local dry cleaner.

"Would it be a good job for her?" Mohammad asked the friend who told them about it.

"Yes, yes," his friend said. "They are good people. It is a good place to work."

Mohammad thought for a moment. "What about me? Could I go too?"

"Okay," his friend said. "Sure. I don't know why not."

Mohammad and Moradi went to work. This was an immense relief to him. He started in September, and by the end of the month, he was able to be financially self-sufficient.

In his house hangs a certificate. There are not many pictures on their walls, but this particular certificate hangs in a prominent place. At the top, his name is written in large, bold letters, and beneath that it reads, "CWS recognizes that he has successfully achieved self-sufficiency within 180 days of arrival in Lancaster, Pennsylvania. He has demonstrated hard work and dedication throughout this time of transition."

On a different wall, he hung the lanyard he wore when they first arrived in New York. Its string clings to a small pin pushed into the wall above their front door, as if he does not want to

forget where they have come from. As if he does not want Moradi
and the boys to forget what it was like when they first landed.

To Whom It May Concern:
My name is: Mohammad.
I am a refugee from: Syria.

23

The Good City

November 2017

We are off to Philadelphia again, this time early in the morning. Mohammad, with the help of his dentist, has arranged for insurance to cover his dental work. He will need at least four or five visits to have everything completed, and by the end of it all he should have a new mouth, a new smile. I'm excited for him. Something about this seems to mark his arrival in the US with hope. It will be good for him in many ways—eating, confidence, maybe even in getting a better job.

I drive south through the city. It's sunny and cold, the first week of November. I pull up outside Mohammad's house and wait in the car. He peeks through the front door, motions that he'll just be a minute, then vanishes again. When he reappears, Moradi trails behind him. He climbs into the passenger seat and Moradi gets in the back.

"Good morning," I say.

"Good morning, Shawn," he says. He's in very good spirits. He has been waiting for this dental work for a long time.

Moradi smiles. "Hello," she says shyly.

"Ready to have some teeth pulled?" I ask Mohammad, laughing.

"Ah, yes." He grimaces, shaking his head.

"Moradi, you are coming along today?"

She nods.

"She has an appointment as well," he says. "A checkup."

"Okay," I say, plugging the Philadelphia address into my phone's GPS. "Let's go."

I ask him about the boys, how school is going, if they're making friends. "Have you had any luck yet getting the bus situation sorted out? Has the school district added your house to their route?"

He shakes his head. "Oh well. We are fine."

"Still no bus," I say, amazed at the inefficiency of our school system. "Is your oldest still riding his bike to school?"

Suddenly he becomes animated. "Shawn! You will not believe this. Someone stole his bike off our back patio!" He is laughing in amazement and surprise.

"Did you keep it locked?"

"Yes! Yes, of course we locked it. We came out in the morning and it was gone."

I shake my head and sigh. "Mohammad, someone stole my bike last year. That's frustrating."

He's still laughing about it, as though the shock is new to him. When he talks, it's as if he's making a plea to the person who stole his bike—he's sincere and animated.

"This bicycle, right now we need it! My son needs it! If I didn't need it, I'd tell them, 'Here, come to me, I will give you this bike.'

But we need it. My son needs it to go to school every day." He falls back in the seat, sighing, shrugging. "Ah well. What can I do?"

By the time he tells me the bike story, we have left the city behind us. First we ease our way through the suburbs, trees everywhere, and then we're into the farmland, the rolling hills with occasional houses dotting the landscape.

"I told Moradi, if we live out here close to you, we can meet every day, morning and evening." He chuckles. "Look, Shawn, look! Look at those two houses. Side by side. Like that. We can sit outside and drink coffee. We can play. The children can play. We can do anything here! Not like the city. The boys can run and ride bikes."

Moradi laughs in the back seat. She seems to find Mohammad's never-ending optimism amusing.

"Do people steal bikes in Syria?" I ask him.

"Yes, yes." His words are clipped, as if he's already accepted it as part of his life and moved on. "But here? I am surprised. I didn't think these things happened here. My brother-in-law, he had two bicycles stolen. He locked them and still they are gone. Two times."

Moradi is clearly tired, and she doesn't say much. The sun shines brightly in the window, and she pulls her covering over her face and leans sideways against the headrest. I often wonder what she's thinking, how she views this country that is now her home. I wonder if she's making friends, learning English. It can't be an easy transition.

"Mohammad, what did you do for work when you lived in Syria?" I ask. "I know you told me once you used to drive in Kuwait, right?"

"Yes, I worked in Kuwait for many years."

"Did you fly there or drive there?"

"Sometimes each. Sometimes drive, sometimes fly. The drive was around 1,500 kilometers, and we couldn't go through Iraq in those days. We went from Syria to Jordan to Saudi Arabia to Kuwait."

I try to picture driving through those Middle Eastern countries, passing through various border guards, just to get to a country where I could make a living.

"Before this war in Syria, we never went to Iraq. Never. We were not allowed. Bashar said that, and it was printed in our passports. 'Do not go to Iraq.' If you went, you were in big problems."

"What kind of work did you do?"

"In Kuwait, I did many things. Many different things. I drove truck. I drove taxi. I worked for a rental car company. In Kuwait, it was much better to work because of the exchange rate. One time I stayed there for five years before going home. I was twenty years old when I first traveled there to work."

"What was it like, working there?"

"It was good. The money was good."

"So, when did you meet Moradi, if you spent so much time in Kuwait?"

He laughs quietly. "I had a friend there from Lebanon, and he wanted to see Syria. 'Okay, no problem,' I told him. So the next time I went home, he came with me. I showed him around my village. We stayed for one month, and our time came to return to Kuwait to go back to work. We were getting ready to leave, to drive back through Jordan, when my friend came to me and said my mother was very upset. He said she wanted me to get married, that it wasn't good for her to be so sad. He told me mothers should not have to cry like that. What could I do? I didn't know what to do. He told me my mother said she has a girl for me, that I needed to go to this girl's house to see if I liked her. If I did, I could marry her. If not, we would go back to Kuwait."

"Really?" I ask, laughing.

"Yes!" he says. "I told him, 'Fine. Let's go.' But I knew I wouldn't like her. We went to my home, and then my mother went with me to Moradi's house. We spent some time there with her and her family."

"So, what happened?" I prod.

He grins. "I went back to where my friend was staying. 'What happened?' he asked me. I said, 'I am ready to get married. I have to marry this girl.'" He laughs and slaps his leg. Moradi stirs in the back of the car.

"What did your friend say?"

"He was shocked. 'What?' he said. I told him again that I would like to get married, so he said okay and went back to Kuwait without me."

"How long were you engaged?"

"We met on the fifth of January and we were married two weeks later, on the nineteenth."

"What? That's fast! What are weddings like in Syria?"

"Weddings are huge celebrations. Very happy. The wedding was so beautiful. Everyone from the village came out and everyone was dancing and singing. It starts in the evening with lots of singing and eating good food. The next day we meet again around lunchtime. The men are all dressed in white. We dance and sing and celebrate all day. You should see it." He pauses. "Wait."

He pulls out his phone and brings up a video of a wedding that took place in his village not too long ago. A jubilance is there that

I have not seen at any American wedding. The men are all up and dancing in a line around the large room, hundreds of them. The children run among them here and there. Their voices are loud and chanting, and they move in groups. It seems to go on and on forever.

"That is my village," Mohammad says in a wistful voice. "That is a wedding in my village."

We drive on quietly for a few minutes, the miles passing. We get closer to Philadelphia, and the morning traffic gathers around us. The sun glares from the east through a sky low with wispy white clouds. The car engine drones on as if it could go on forever. For some reason I am very aware of the fact that we are being propelled along at sixty-five miles per hour. When you speak with someone about their hike through the wilderness—or their long, slow movement to the United States, a journey that took them years—any fast movement stands out as remarkable.

For a moment Mohammad stares out the passenger window, seemingly captured by the busyness, the unceasing movement.

Moradi pipes up from the back seat. "Mohammad, he needs another wife," she says with a smile in her voice. Her face is still hidden behind her covering, but she pulls it aside and says it again, in case we didn't hear or understand. "Mohammad, he needs another wife."

I laugh. "Is that true, Mohammad?"

But before I can even get the question out of my mouth, he is protesting. "No, no, no! I do not need another wife."

"Do many people have more than one wife in your village?" I ask.

He shrugs. "Not many. Only a few. The very rich."

"But it's okay for that to happen? It's okay for men to have more than one wife in Syria, where you lived?"

He takes on the air of someone trying to explain something to a child, something complex that they may not understand. "People misunderstand the prophet," he says, thinking through his words, trying to find the right English to explain what he wants to say. "The prophet Muhammad? He said you can have more than one wife, but he also said . . . Oh, what's the word . . ."

He fiddles with his phone, working the translation app, then shows me the screen.

"Justice?" I say.

"Yes, justice. If you have more than one wife, you must have justice."

"You mean, you have to be fair?"

"Yes. Fair. Justice. But you can't be fair! It's not possible! Now, if you smile, Shawn, if you have two wives and you smile at one but not at the other, that's a problem. That is not justice. Because of this, you should not marry more than one wife. Justice."

"Justice," I say, grinning.

Moradi laughs.

"Justice," Mohammad says, sincere in his affection.

"Justice," I say quietly to myself. Then louder, to him: "Are there tribes in Syria?"

He doesn't catch my meaning at first. I try to think of other ways of saying it.

"You know. Sunni? Shia? Is your village one of those groups?"

"Ah! Yes! Okay, Shawn. Before the war, in my village, I didn't know who was who. I lived, that was all. We all lived. My village is Sunni. Over the way is the Christian village. Another village might be Shia. But when we would all be together, I could not tell who was Christian, who was Sunni, who was Shia. That never happened before the war, calling people by their religion, their tribe. No one cared. But now people are here and here and here, divided. This is the problem. Before the war, no. In my area lives every tribe. There is every tribe."

He raises his eyebrows as if to see if I understand. I nod.

"But now it is all different. Before the war, we ate together, laughed together. Now, if you see someone, everyone comments on what they are. 'Oh, that person is Shia,' or, 'Oh, that person is Sunni.' This is not good. This is just since the war. People no longer trust this person, that person."

He is quiet for a moment. I can tell he's thinking about this new development.

"It is no different, these groups. God is God."

I find it interesting he would say that. I wonder if this is a view held by most Muslims or if Mohammad is in the minority.

This is where the language barrier keeps us from going deeper, and I sense it with many topics, not just religion. I'd love to know more about what he believes, more about the religion he grew up with, but when I ask tentative questions, we have trouble making the connection. He doesn't understand what I'm trying to ask. We talk more about his wedding, his boys.

We drive on in silence—not an uncomfortable one, but the kind that occasionally settles into a car when friends are on a long trip. I yawn. Moradi says something in Arabic. Mohammad laughs.

"What?" I ask. "Moradi, what did you say?"

Mohammad translates. "Moradi says you need to get some sleep."

"It's all my children," I say. "Mohammad, my kids keep me up at night."

———

We enter Philadelphia with its endless row homes and inter-sections and cars. Off in the distance, Center City rises, a glass metropolis gleaming in the morning sun. I have driven those downtown streets many times, usually at night, picking up and dropping off customers. It is not an easy place to drive—there are few good places along those busy streets for picking people up or dropping them off. It can be hard to find a person in that mass of humanity, especially on a weekend night when the streets are pulsing with people.

I back into a parking space across from the dentist and put all of my change into the meter. Moradi donates a few dollars in quarters to the cause, and we go into the dentist's office. After Mohammad checks in and I say hello to the dentist, I walk back across the road to a diner, where I will do some work while Moradi and Mohammad have their teeth worked on.

I sit at a table along the window, writing, thinking about every-thing Mohammad has told me about Syria and his life there. I think about how much he loves the farmland outside of the city, how he always proclaims it is just like Syria.

My own life has been so simple—I travel when I want to travel, move when I want to move. I have lived abroad and have not always lived close to family, but that was my choice. My decision. Moham-mad, on the other hand, was a man without a country for four long years, a man the world was trying to decide what to do with.

Then the world sent him here.

———

I see Mohammad come outside, so I leave the diner and go over to him. He is holding bags of Arabic flatbread, the kind he and his family live on, the kind they have with every meal.

"How are you?" I ask. "How do you feel?"

He winces, raises a hand to his cheek. "Okay." He shrugs. "So-so."

Moradi comes out, and the three of us walk to the car. He loads the bread into the back seat, and Moradi slides in on the other side. We head for home.

"How did it go?" I ask. "How many teeth did he take out?"

"Five," he says, again wincing. His cheek is puffed out like a chipmunk's, the side of his mouth packed full of gauze.

"Did it hurt?"

He nods. He reaches into his pocket and pulls out a bottle of pills, popping the lid. He swallows a few. I offer him water but he shakes his head, pointing again at his cheek stuffed with gauze.

"Do you have to work today?"

"They said I could let them know. I thought I would go in, but now I don't know."

We drive on, this time in silence. Moradi drifts off. The city retreats, replaced again by countryside. Tree branches reach out over the road, and then the landscape opens up into farmers' rolling fields, the corn cut to a tan stubble, the tobacco long gone, the soybean fields golden and ready for harvest. Then it is all trees again, and long lanes leading to houses in the shadows.

Mohammad begins talking again, and I can tell by the wooziness of his voice and the wistfulness of his words that the medication is taking effect. I can't help but grin as he drifts into a drugged kind of sentimentality. I'm his best friend now, and the United States is his kingdom.

"Shawn," he says in a floating voice, "I am not nervous when I ride with you. No. Not at all. In Syria and Jordan and even here when I ride with people, I am like this." He grips the armrests with terrified hands. "But with you, I am relaxed. I am not nervous."

"Well, thank you," I say.

We drive through a small town. Sidewalks line the street, but no one is outside.

"Where are all the people?" he asks, desperation in his voice. "Where is everyone? I think this a lot here in your country. Are all of these houses empty?"

"No, they're not empty. We just don't go out very much. We stay in our houses, and when we leave, we get in our cars and drive away."

"It is interesting to me. I never see people. Only empty streets. Empty sidewalks. Where are all the people?"

He is somewhere else now, his mind drifting from this thing to that.

"When is your next appointment?" I ask.

"In one week. He will take out six more teeth. Then he can take a model of my mouth, and then I can eat lamb again." He laughs quietly, almost to himself.

"I will be in North Carolina for Thanksgiving," I say. "I won't be able to take you to your appointment. Can someone else drive you? Or do you think you can do it without getting lost?"

"North Carolina? Why are you always going away?"

I smile. "It does seem that way, doesn't it. Do you need me to find someone to take you to Philadelphia?"

"No, no. We will see. I can drive."

We come in through the south side of Lancaster, over the bridge that seems to mark the entrance to the city from that direction. By now it is early afternoon. The river curves beneath us, moving ever on, first to the Susquehanna, then to the Chesapeake, and finally to the Atlantic. All connected.

"I can't believe what happened in Texas," he says. Only a few days before, a shooter entered a church in Sutherland Springs, Texas, killing twenty-six people. The normal outrage ensued about guns and violence and what seems to have become the new normal in our country. Not too long before that, it was Las Vegas.

"It's awful," I say, interested that this would be something on his mind.

"I know these things happen. Even in my country, they happen. Maybe if it happens in the street, I am not surprised, but in a church? This is very, very bad to happen there. Very bad."

He sighs. We turn onto his street.

"So, now that you've been to Philadelphia, would you rather live there?" I ask him.

"No, no. This is a good city," he says. "I like it here. This is better. It is smaller."

We pull up in front of his house. He sighs again.

"Yes, I like it here."

24

Through Trees
and Shadows

November 2017

There are days when I wonder if this world can continue to exist under the current load of hate and misunderstanding and evil, when I wonder if the hearts of all people can somehow find an antidote to racism and virulent nationalism and a concern only for ourselves. We are born to these things as the sparks fly upward, I suppose. I know I am. My friendship with Mohammad has been both the diagnosis and the beginning of a cure in me.

But there are other days too, days like today, when I'm standing in a park on a sunny day, warm for this time of year, and my children are laughing and shouting, and I'm waiting for Mohammad and his family to arrive. He calls me, asks where I am. Long's Park is a large place, and the road that goes through it loops in on itself.

Besides that, it seems like most of the city has decided to come out to play, and people are everywhere. Cars drive slowly past.

I tell him where I am, using the pond as a landmark, and start walking toward where he says he is. This is the perfect metaphor for our friendship. It feels like we are constantly trying to find each other. I see Mohammad and Moradi from across the way, their four boys tumbling out of the van behind them like puppies in open space for the first time. They laugh and throw pinecones at each other and hide under benches. The youngest stops for a moment and stares at the water, and I can tell it is one of the great struggles of his life, not jumping into that pond.

"Mohammad!" I shout across the water. He turns, smiles, and waves. Moradi nods bashfully. They walk around the edge, and so do I, and gradually we meet each other somewhere in between.

"Come," I say, motioning for them to follow, and we walk together back to where my family has set up camp in the park. I give the introductions. This is my father, my mother, my aunt, my grandmother. This is Mohammad, Moradi, and their boys.

My father shakes Mohammad's hand, then reaches for Moradi's. She declines politely, and I explain to my dad that traditional Muslim women do not shake a man's hand. These are the tiny, awkward steps in a friendship like this. These are the things you learn on the fly, and you can let the intricacies discourage you, or you can laugh at yourself and learn from them. This is what happens in the collision of cultures, when people move 6,000 miles from home. We have to be patient with each other, all of us.

We bring out the pizzas and snacks and water, and everyone eats. My Iraqi friend and translator, Bilal, is there too, and he pulls a plastic container out of a paper grocery sack. When he opens it, an incredible smell escapes.

"This is a traditional Iraqi dish," he says, smiling. Mohammad and Moradi see something in that food that speaks to them of home. Moradi's eyes light up—she has not touched the pizza, but this new food has her attention. They reach in with their hands, suddenly home. We all eat it with our fingers. This is community. This is friendship.

Soon my children are kicking a soccer ball with Mohammad's children. My wife invites Moradi over to a circle of lawn chairs that includes my mom, my grandmother, and my aunt. I watch them for a moment, these women of different ages, different continents. Moradi wears a dress and a head scarf. I listen in while she answers questions. She looks for the right English word the way you might carefully choose a piece of fruit from a pile. The other women listen and nod, and my wife is there to nudge her along or help her find a word.

The women smile and laugh quietly. No matter how different they are, they share many of the same concerns, the same hopes. I hear them all laugh again, and I wonder what it is that keeps us frightened of each other.

"Do you want to have more children?" one of the women asks Moradi. I can tell Moradi isn't sure what she's asking.

Maile points to her own stomach, makes a round motion, and says, "Have another baby?"

Moradi smiles. "Only if they can promise me a girl," she says. Everyone laughs.

One of Mohammad's boys throws a football to my son Sam. It's an awkward throw—he's probably never thrown a football before. But his eyes sparkle with the joy of doing something new, and my son scampers off to retrieve the ball and toss it back. Mohammad's son catches the ball on the first try, and everyone cheers.

Mohammad is peppered with questions, and he seems to enjoy it.

"What is the weather like in Syria?"

"What do you eat?"

"Where did you work?"

In the background, the sounds of a city park carry on, and Bilal chimes in from time to time in order to translate or correct. I wonder if my father has ever spoken to a Muslim man before. I wonder if my mother has ever shared a laugh with a Syrian.

A few of my relatives and friends have no problem with a refugee ban. They believe danger lurks in the hearts of these landless, homeless people. I realize, perhaps for the first time, that they might be correct. It is possible that in the midst of 60,000 refugees entering the United States, there could be one bad apple. There could be someone who has been so bent by the pain in their life that they want to seek some kind of revenge.

It is possible.

But should our fear of that one keep us from providing refuge to thousands like Mohammad and his family? Are there enough restrictions or safeguards in the world for us to put in place that will guarantee, 100 percent, that nothing bad will happen to us? Even then, evil already lurks among us, as we have seen so many times before. In the face of this evil, should we not provide refuge for families like Mohammad's?

Should our fear overpower our love?

It's time to go. The sun dips in the west and darkness creeps in over the eastern edge of the park. It is chilly. We gather our children and our soccer balls and our footballs and our lawn chairs.

We throw away the pizza boxes and argue about who will take Bilal's leftovers home. Eventually we figure out how to split the spoils among us. Blankets are folded. We are all tired in a good way. Mohammad shakes everyone's hand, says "thank you" a thousand times. He drinks up new friendships. He inhales them, and his eyes sparkle. Every time I introduce him to someone new, he acts as though they are a long-lost friend, someone he now holds in the highest esteem.

Moradi nods a kind smile to the men and embraces each of the women one at a time, slowly, savoring the new friendships.

Mohammad's boys are already off and running through the park toward their old minivan, crossing the large expanse of grass. He turns to me, almost vehement in his affection.

"Thank you, Shawn," he says, pumping my hand in a vigorous handshake. "Thank you. Next time we have your family to our house. Next time we have everyone over."

"Of course," I say. "That sounds great."

Moradi, walking away, turns and shouts something to him in Arabic. He looks over, and their youngest boy is far in the distance.

He shouts the boy's name and turns, giving us one final wave, then chases his youngest son through the park.

"Good-bye, Mohammad!" I say. "Good-bye, Moradi! Good-bye, boys!"

I go back to my family. They talk about how friendly Mohammad and his wife are. There is a heaviness weighing on all of us after hearing some of what he's been through. We gather our things, walk quietly to our vehicles, and say good-bye to each other.

We drive slowly out of the park, through the trees and the shadows, back onto the street that leads into the heart of the city.

25

Once We Were Strangers

November 2017

I'm sitting in a coffee shop west of Charlotte, North Carolina, where my family and I go every year to celebrate Thanksgiving with my wife's parents and brothers and extended family. In some ways, this place reminds me of where I grew up in Pennsylvania—the sky is a flat gray, and the patches of blue that leak through are disinterested, distant. The air is chilly this time of year, though not as cold as Pennsylvania. Rolling hills are covered in forests, and the highways span creeks and rivers. But everyone's accent reminds me we are several hundred miles from where I grew up. I can't help but feel a little bit like an outsider when I'm here.

The bustle of the holiday season is in full effect. The stores advertise their upcoming sales while everyone races around, preparing for the feast to come. Santa peeks out from every corner. My wife's family prepares to travel in from other parts of North Carolina and Tennessee. This is something at the forefront of my mind since I met Mohammad, the fact that we can travel so far to see each other and celebrate in peace. There are no checkpoints as we cross from state to state. There is no threat of bombing.

I do not have to worry about whether or not my house will be there when I get home.

I remember Mohammad sitting on my porch earlier this year, reflecting on Eid, talking about how his family and friends would be together. Again I'm reminded of the cost refugees pay when they flee from their homes. These decisions are never made lightly. As Mohammad said, "No one ever wants to leave their home. But we had no choice."

It would seem we are obsessed with returning people to the land of their birth or keeping them "where they belong." I think about the words of the poem "The New Colossus," inscribed inside the base of the Statue of Liberty. I wonder if they apply to our nation anymore.

> Give me your tired, your poor,
> Your huddled masses yearning to breathe free,
> The wretched refuse of your teeming shore.
> Send these, the homeless, tempest-tossed to me,
> I lift my lamp beside the golden door!

I often think of the certificate on Mohammad's wall, the one he displays so proudly, the one that verifies he was financially self-sufficient within 180 days.

"It was sooner than that," he always says when I ask him about it. "We took less than ninety days."

26

When Are You Coming Back?

November 2017

One year has passed since I met Mohammad, since I walked into the hubbub of language at Church World Service and spoke with this Syrian man by way of a translator. I think of all the things we did this year: looking for houses, meeting for coffee, traveling to Philadelphia for his dentist appointments. I think of all the things this year has taught me about refugees, about Muslims, about friendship. It's hard to believe it has just been one year. After everything Mohammad has been through, I would imagine he feels much the same way. After all, he has gotten a job in a foreign country, enrolled his children in school, passed his driver's test, learned a new language, and made new friends. He's looked for a different home, has found a dentist, and nearly has new teeth.

I was sad to leave him for this trek south. I would have loved to have celebrated Thanksgiving with him, to see his boys' eyes widen at the turkey and the food and the parade, to hear Moradi and Maile talking quietly about work or raising children or giving that driver's test another try. But Mohammad cannot afford to take off work long enough to get to Charlotte, nearly five hundred miles away. So we have to settle for talking on the phone or sending texts.

"You seem to have forgotten me!" he texted me the other day.

"I thought you were the one who forgot me!" I replied, joking. The days have passed quickly.

"How could I forget who I love, but I thought you were busy."

He is such a kind man. His message made me smile.

I am reminded of the time I spent in Istanbul, Turkey, where the men walk from here to there linking arms, or how they sit close together. I picture Mohammad and his boys, especially his youngest, how sometimes when they are playfully arguing, their faces are so close together that they are breathing the same air. Mohammad isn't this way with me, but he exhibits a certain kindness, an underlying gentleness that is absent from most of my other male friendships.

When I last spoke with him on the phone a few days ago, he told me of his trip to Philadelphia for his most recent dental appointment. He drove himself and Moradi on his own.

"Did you get lost?" I asked, impressed.

"No! I did not get lost. But I was so tired after the appointment. He pulled six more teeth, and I was so tired."

"Six teeth! Wow! But you made it there and home without getting lost?" I said, thinking back through the twists and turns of the route. "Well done."

"What can I do?" He chuckled. "I went the way you showed me. It was okay."

There was a moment of silence on the phone, a blip in the conversation. Just as I was about to ask if he was still there, he spoke.

"When are you coming back, Shawn?"

"I'll be home in about a week," I told him. "Not too long now."

"Good," he said. "That is good."

———

We are finally home from North Carolina, and because it's almost winter and I'm in between writing contracts, I'm driving for Uber and Lyft again. The days are short, and it feels like most of the time I'm driving at night, through the dark, on rain-slicked streets that reflect headlights and brake lights in long streaks.

The people I drive during this time of year seem different, quieter, more reflective. I haven't done any kind of official tally, but it seems to me that people look out the window more than usual, watch the streetlights, ponder the city buildings and the empty windows. There is something somber about the dark weeks between Thanksgiving and Christmas, something slow and melancholy.

On one of the bright blue days, one of our first days back north, I go to see Mohammad where he works. I'm excited to see him.

There are no customers in the shop, and for a moment I don't see any employees either, but then, through the racks of hanging clothes, Mohammad emerges.

"Shawn!" he exclaims. It's been about three weeks since I've seen him, and he greets me with a hug.

"How are you, my friend?" I ask, and then, when I get a good look at him, "Mohammad! What happened to your teeth?"

His mouth is empty of teeth. He grins, then grimaces.

"It's the insurance," he says. "The dentist, he pulled all of my teeth, and then the insurance said they would not cover it. So I am waiting for a new insurance card before I can have the rest of the work done. It should come tomorrow."

His mouth looks soft and sensitive, and without teeth he looks much older. He doesn't even look like the same person.

"Mohammad, I'm sorry. I hope you can have it taken care of soon."

He laughs and waves his hand. "What can you do?"

We catch up for a few minutes about our families and work. I tell him I'll stop by his house one of these nights while I'm driving.

"How late do you work this afternoon?" I ask.

"We are leaving soon. Moradi is taking her driver's test."

"She is? Yes! Let me know how it goes."

"I will text you if she passes."

Customers are lining up at the front of the dry cleaner.

"I'm going to head out," I tell him.

"No, Shawn! Stay! Sit!"

I smile. "Mohammad, you're busy. I should go and let you work. I'll see you soon."

He finally relents, and I walk toward the door.

"Good-bye, Shawn!" Moradi calls from the other side of the room. Her English sounds better, even after just a few weeks.

"Good-bye," I say. "Good luck!"

———

When I think about the book I set out to write a year ago and compare it with the book I have written, I sometimes wonder if anyone will read it. I thought this book would perhaps be an action-adventure tale following a Syrian family through bombs and bullets to an inner-city US neighborhood that persecuted them for being Muslim. I thought it might be the tale of how a middle-aged man in search of meaning helped a Syrian family find the American dream.

The book I thought I might write embarrasses me now.

Instead, I wrote a book in which, at first glance, nothing happens. At least not on the outside. I feel like I should have a disclaimer on the cover: "No one was harmed in the creation of this book." But something was harmed. Something happened.

My belief that refugees have little to offer was crushed. My belief that they need my help more than they need my friendship was brought low. My deep-seated, hidden concern that every Muslim person might be inherently violent or dedicated to the destruction of the West was exposed and found to be false.

These two books—the book I planned to write and the book I have actually written—are as dissimilar as the relationship I thought I would have with Mohammad and the one I actually have. When I decided to reach out to Mohammad, when I decided to "help," I envisioned taking his family food or finding them furniture they needed or emailing him the address of the DMV. The help I was prepared to offer was help given at arm's length, aid that would cost me perhaps a tiny bit of time and maybe a few dollars but not much more than that.

But I, not Mohammad, needed more than that. Actually, it turns out we both needed the same thing. We both needed a friend.

———

Who is my neighbor?

Friendship is such a strange, unexpected thing. It can creep up on you when you least expect it, from the least likely places.

I never could have imagined I'd become friends with a Syrian man from 6,000 miles away, a Muslim man whose children call him Abba.

In the last year, Mohammad has changed my life in ways difficult to explain or describe. The coffee, the drives to Philadelphia, the chats on my front porch.

There's one thing I know for sure. If you insert me into the story of the good Samaritan, I'm not only the good Samaritan; I'm not only the one who stopped to help. I'm also the man lying along the side of the road, beaten down. I'm the one dying from selfishness and hypervigilance and fear.

The role of the good Samaritan, in a role reversal I couldn't have seen coming, has been taken on by Mohammad.

Before I even knew him, he called me friend.

Postscript

February 11, 2018

I am with Maile and the kids in Charlotte, visiting her parents. I had a meeting with a potential client in Nashville, and we decided to make a trip of it. The weather is warm here, warmer than in Lancaster. The last two days have been gray skies and clouds, and the air carries hints of spring.

We were all sitting around the dining table the other night when I got a text. I took my phone out of my pocket and saw a picture of Mohammad giving a grin in which he was baring all of his teeth. That's right. His teeth. After months and months, he finally has teeth again! I can't wait to see him in person.

He sent me another text, this time a one-liner. "Finally Moradi succeeded."

So much good news in one weekend. Moradi passed her driver's test. Now she can work or go out in the evening if she wants, and Mohammad won't have to leave the boys to pick her up. Or he can work later at the dry cleaner and she can go home to be there when the boys return from school. It's a new kind of flexibility that will give them much more freedom in their life.

Finally it feels like things are coming together for them. The next step is to find them both new, better-paying jobs. And maybe in the summer we can find him that home in the country he's wanted.

———

I stayed with a friend not long ago, and I stood at her patio door looking out at the backs of the neighbors' houses behind hers. I asked her what her neighborhood was like, and she said it was mostly good, but a Muslim family had moved in behind them. It made her nervous, she said, looking out and seeing the woman in her head covering. She was afraid of what they might do.

"I'm sure it's fine," she said, "but you see all these things in the news. You just never know. You can't be too careful."

I would agree, but with a different response. We can't be too careful, true. We have to pull out all the stops in welcoming the refugee and the immigrant, in getting to know those who live around us, in showing love to our neighbors. We can't afford to isolate people anymore. We can't afford to push folks to the fringes of our society.

This world we've created is a product of isolationism and fear, distrust and anger.

———

Mohammad left a comment on my Facebook page the other day. "How I wish your home to be next to my home," he wrote.

I think of my friend, the one who is frightened by the Muslim woman living in the house behind hers. What I wouldn't give to have Mohammad living in the house behind mine! I know now what I was missing out on before I met him—what all of us miss out on when we don't reach out to our neighbors. The sitting down together, the coffee, the sharing of stories. The community.

Not long ago, Mohammad and I were strangers. Now we are friends. This, it seems to me, is no small deal in a world and a system that would prefer we fear one another. This, it seems to me, is the first step in bringing a lasting peace.

Discussion Questions

1. Have you ever looked at the world around you and felt the urge to take action? When did you sense this? What actions came to mind?

2. Name friends who encourage you to step outside of your comfort zone. Make concrete plans to spend time with them soon.

3. What other nationalities are represented in your community? Reach out to one person or family from another country and find out what brought them to your area.

4. Where would you go if a disaster happened in your community? To whom would you look for help?

5. Have you ever been in a foreign culture? How did you feel? What about it appealed to you, and what about it made you feel out of place?

6. How many hours would you have to work in a week to cover your monthly expenses if you made $10 an hour?

7. To which cultures do you feel the most affinity or attraction? What is appealing about them?

8. Which cultures or nations do you fear the most? Why?

9. When you think of the word *Muslim*, what comes to mind?

10. Do you know the names of the people who live closest to you? Why or why not?

11. What about your life has involved the most red tape? Getting a license? Going to college? Buying a home? Who helped you navigate those applications?

12. If you moved to a foreign country where you knew no one and didn't speak the language, where would you begin? What are the first things you would try to do to get settled in?

13. The United States has welcomed immigrants and refugees for generations. When did your family arrive in the US? What language(s) did they speak?

14. What is it about where you live that makes it feel like home? If you had to move away, how would you begin making your new place into a home?

15. What situations have you had in life when you were the good Samaritan, helping others? When were you the one on the side of the road, needing help? When were you the manager of the hotel, watching someone help someone else?

16. Who do you think God might be asking you to become friends with?

Acknowledgments

As it is often noted, a book is much more than the sum effort of one person. This book would not exist without the helpful guidance of my agent, Ruth Samsel; my kind and diligent editors, Kelsey Bowen and Jessica English; and the quiet insistence of my wife, Maile.

But where would I be without Mohammad? His kindness, perseverance, and excitement at sharing his story have inspired me, and his friendship is an unexpected and precious gift.

May we all be so eager to love our neighbors as he is.

Notes

1. "Executive Order Protecting the Nation from Foreign Terrorist Entry into the United States," WhiteHouse.gov, January 27, 2017, https://www.whitehouse.gov/presidential-actions/executive-order-protecting-nation-foreign-terrorist-entry-united-states.

2. Holly Hartman, "Ramadan and Eid al-Fitr," Infoplease, accessed April 3, 2018, https://www.infoplease.com/ramadan-and-eid-al-fitr.

3. Rana F. Sweis, "Jordan Struggles under a Wave of Syrian Refugees," *New York Times*, February 13, 2016, https://www.nytimes.com/2016/02/14/world/middleeast/jordan-syria-refugees.html.

Shawn Smucker is the author of the award-winning novel *The Day the Angels Fell* and its sequel, *The Edge of Over There*. He lives with his wife and six children in Lancaster, Pennsylvania. You can find him online at www.shawnsmucker.com.

COULD IT BE POSSIBLE THAT DEATH IS A GIFT?

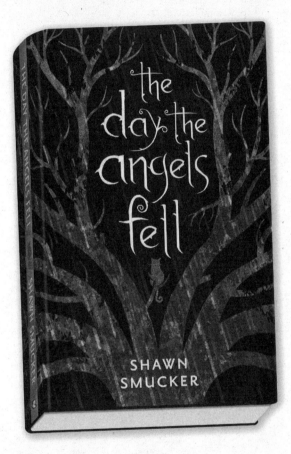

When tragedy shakes young Samuel Chambers's family, his search for answers entangles him in the midst of an ancient conflict and leads him on an unexpected journey to find the Tree of Life.

THE **CAPTIVATING SEQUEL** TO
THE AWARD-WINNING
THE DAY THE ANGELS FELL

Abra Miller carries a secret and a responsibility that she never wanted. When it takes her into a crypt at New Orleans Cemetery No. 1, **will she get out alive?**